Switch

3

Workbook

Nicholas Tims

OXFORD

OXFORD
UNIVERSITY PRESS

Great Clarendon Street, Oxford OX2 6DP

Oxford University Press is a department of the University of Oxford. It furthers the University's objective of excellence in research, scholarship, and education by publishing worldwide in

Oxford New York

Auckland Cape Town Dar es Salaam Hong Kong Karachi Kuala Lumpur Madrid Melbourne Mexico City Nairobi New Delhi Shanghai Taipei Toronto

With offices in

Argentina Austria Brazil Chile Czech Republic France Greece Guatemala Hungary Italy Japan Poland Portugal Singapore South Korea Switzerland Thailand Turkey Ukraine Vietnam

OXFORD and OXFORD ENGLISH are registered trade marks of Oxford University Press in the UK and in certain other countries

First published 2010
2014 2013 2012 2011 2010
10 9 8 7 6 5 4 3 2 1

ISBN: 978 0 19484908 1

Printed in Spain by Orymu S.A.

ACKNOWLEDGEMENTS

Illustrations by: Adrian Barclay pp.21, 39, 57, 61; Paul Daviz pp.15, 33, 43, 51; Kev Hopgood pp.12, 19, 30, 35, 38, 45, 55; Andres Martinez Ricci/The Organisation pp.31, 37, 52

We would also like to thank the following for permission to reproduce the following photographs: Alamy pp.9 (chess/Ben Molyneux People), 9 (photography/Mark Baigent), 10 (piluhin), 18 (Bets LaRue), 23 (Peter Alvey), 24 (handcuffs/John Powell Photographer), 24 (broken window/Jarvell Jardey), 25 (d/foodfolio), 27 (a/Photofusion Picture Library), 27 (c/Fancy), 27 (e/Anthony Hatley), 27 (f/avatra images), 28 (Marion Bull), 31 (b/Directphoto Collection), 31 (d/B.A.E. Inc.), 39 (windsurfing/louise murray), 39 (kayaking/Ronald Karpilo), 39 (bungee jumping/Nick Chaldakov), 39 (rock climbing/i love images), 46 (Picture Partners), 58 (cocoa beans/Mark Girvan), 60 (Johner Images), 85 (yoga/Stockbroker/MBI), 85 (riding/Foto Grebler), 85 (juggling/Fancy), 85 (singing/Jim West), 85 (pottery/IML Image Group Ltd), 85 (knitting/Sally and Richard Greenhill), 89 (prison/Mark Harvey), 89 (cell/67photo), 89 (prisoner/moodboard), 91 (lawn/Geoff du Feu), 91 (hedge/David Askham), 91 (flower bed/Ashley Cooper), 91 (pond/Travel and Landscape UK/Mark Sykes), 91 (fence/Elizabeth Whiting & Associates), 91 (tools/Aled Llywelyn), 91 (lawnmower/The Photolibrary Wales), 91 (hose/Brian Posey), 93 (clumsy/Mike Kemp/RubberBall), 93 (graceful/Erik, Isakson/Tetra Images), 93 (intelligent/Vera Berger/Corbis RF), 93 (adventurous/Kuttig - People), 95 (ambulance/David R. Frazier Photolibrary, Inc.), 95 (first aid kit/Denise Hager/Catchlight Visual Services), 95 (stretcher/IS960/Image Source), 95 (bandage/Tetra Images), 96 (Gregory Wrona), 97 (trolley/Kaktusfactory, Ninprapha Lippert/Bon Appetit), 97 (carrier bag/Lenscap), 97 (cashier/bildagentur-online/begsteiger), 97 (check-out/Ken Welsh), 97 (discount/TunaStyle), 99 (mobile phone recharger/Melissa Ferrari), 99 (projector/Stock Take), 99 (portable hard drive/Malcolm Fairman), 99 (memory stick/DJG Technology), 99 (hard drive/Rex Argent), 101 (raw/foodfolio), 101 (cooked/Richard Wainscoat), 101 (fatty/B.A.E. Inc.), 101 (lean/foodfolio), 101 (ripe/D. Hurst); clipartof.com p.54 (car); Corbis p.58 (pod and hands/Owen Franken); Getty Images pp.4 (Bob Stevens/UpperCut Images), 6 (Ivy Reynolds/Workbook Stock), 9 (dancing/Hans Neleman/Taxi), 9 (magazines/Anne Ackermann/Digital Vision), 13 (Ray Pietro/Photonica), 17 (Jupiterimages/Thinkstock), 25 (b/John Terence Turner/Photographer's Choice), 25 (e/Dan Kenyon), 27 (b/Ann Summa/Workbook Stock), 31 (c/Kevin Cooley/Taxi), 31 (e/Elea Dumas/Workbook Stock), 36 (Terje Rakke/The Image Bank), 39 (snorkelling/Charles Gullung/Photonica), 39 (skydiving/Digital Vision), 39 (waterskiing/Bill LoshTaxi), 41 (homework/Somos/Veer), 41 (mountain/Melissa McManus/Stone), 41 (shopping/Jose Luis Pelaez Inc/Blend Images), 41 (argument/Erin Patrice O'Brien/Stone+), 41 (mistake/Glow Images), 54 (light bulb/Stockbyte), 57 (chips/Michael Rosenfeld/Photographer's Choice), 58 (chocolate/National Geographic), 62 (Image Source), 85 (drama/Jupiterimages/Comstock Images), 85 (hiking/Ken Chernus/Taxi), 86 (Andersen Ross/Photodisc), 87 (miserable/Pascal Crapet/Stone), 87 (shocked/B2M Productions/Photographer's Choice RF), 87 (annoyed/Flamingo Photography), 87 (amazed/Chris Ryan/OJO Images), 87 (stressed/Patrick Ryan/Lifesize), 87 (worried/Keith Brofsky/Photodisc), 88 (George Diebold/The Image Bank), 89 (judge/Peter Dazeley/Photographer's Choice RF), 89 (handcuffs/Brand X Pictures), 89 (court/Comstoc), 89 (jury/PNC/Photodisc), 89 (witness/Stockbyte), 90 (Nikolaevich/Taxi), 92 (Caco Vaccaro/Flickr), 93 (dishonest/David Young-Wolff/Stone), 93 (rude/Image Source), 94 (Stephen Alvarez/National Geographic), 95 (broken arm/Ebby May/Taxi), 95 (paramedics/Hans Neleman/Stone), 95 (compress/Michael Nemeth/The Image Bank), 95 (plaster/Creative Crop/Digital Vision), 97 (counter/Somos/Veer), 97 (basket/Dave Rudkin/Dorling Kindersley), 97 (receipt/Comstock), 98 (ML Harris/Iconica), 101 (unripe/Stockbyte); iStockphoto.com p.100 (ShyMan); LifeStraw® p.54 (LifeStraw/(© Vestergaard Frandsen); Press Association Images pp.40 (Corrado Giambalvo/AP), 42 (Philip Shearer/AP); Photolibrary.com pp.8 (HIRB/Index Stock Imagery), 9 (cooking/ulrich niehoff/imagebroker.net), 31 (f/Ulrich Niehoff/imagebroker.net), 39 (kite surfing/Norbert Eisele-Hein/imagebroker.net), 48 (Boutet Jean-Pierre/Oredia), 57 (beef/Tim Hill/Fresh Food Images), 57 (cheese/Tetra Images), 57 (sushi/PureStock), 57 (pasta/Glow Cuisine), 84 (David Davis/Index Stock Imagery), 101 (fresh/David Marsden/Fresh Food Images), 101 (frozen/Joy Skipper/Fresh Food Images); Royalty-free pp.5 (Digital Vision), 9 (music/Radius Images), 25 (a/Photodisc), 25 (c/Digital Vision), 27 (d/Digital Vision), 31 (a), 57 (chicken/MIXA), 99 (remote control/Stockbyte), 99 (disc drive/Photodisc)

Contents

Welcome

Reading

1 **Do you know the people next door to your house or flat?**

Hi Andy,

Are you in your new house? Tell me about it!

There are some new people in your old house. And I've got good news – there's a boy my age, so I've got a friend next door again!

The boy's name is Tom. He's nice. We're going bowling tomorrow. He hasn't got any brothers or sisters.

Write soon – I miss you!

Maisie x

Hi Maisie,

Our new house is big. There are bedrooms for my parents, my sister and me. My new bedroom is enormous! (I'm sending you a photo of it.) The living room is quite small and there's also a small garden. There are two girls next door, Jess and Samantha. There aren't any boys ☹. Jess is our age but Samantha is only nine. I'm meeting them tomorrow. We're having dinner with them.

Andy

2 ★ **Read the emails. Answer the questions. Write Maisie or Andy.**

Who is in a new house? Andy

1 Who has got a new friend? Maisie

2 Who is going bowling tomorrow? Maisie

3 Who has a big bedroom? Andy

3 ★★ **Are the sentences true or false? Write T or F.**

Maisie and Andy live next door to each other. F

1 Maisie and Tom are the same age. T

2 Tom's got a sister. F

3 Andy's got a big bedroom. T

4 There aren't any boys next door to Andy. T

5 Samantha is the same age as Andy. F

4 ★★★ **Answer the questions.**

What is Maisie's good news?
There is a boy her age next door.

1 What does Maisie think about Tom?
She thinks he's nice.

2 What is she doing with him tomorrow?
She's going bowling with him tomorrow.

3 How many bedrooms are there in Andy's new house?
Three.

4 What is the name of the older girl next door to Andy?
Jess.

5 What is Andy's family doing tomorrow?
Andy's family is having dinner with the people next door tomorrow.

Revision

1 ★ Cross out the words that don't match.

MP3 player netbook ~~ferry~~

1 lake ~~businesswoman~~ waterfall

2 ~~valley~~ lorry tram

3 read comics take photos ~~postal worker~~

4 ~~watch videos~~ police officer hairdresser

2 ★ Write the words that don't match in exercise 1 next to the right topics.

vehicles *ferry*

1 geographical features valley

2 jobs postal worker, businesswoman

3 fun activities watch videos

3 ★★ Complete the crossword.

		1 W			2 L					
		3 A	S	S	I	S	T	A	N	T
		I			F					
		T		4 N	E	T	B	O	O	K
		E			G					
		R			U					
	5 L				A			6 D		
7 C	A	M	C	O	R	D	E	R		
	K				D			I		
8 F	E	R	R	Y				V		
								E		
						9 L	O	R	R	Y

1 This person works in a restaurant

2 A job in a sports centre

3 A job in a shop: a shop …

4 A small computer

5 An area of water

6 This person works in a car: a taxi …

7 A video camera

8 A type of boat

9 A large vehicle with wheels

4 ★★ Complete the hobbies.

I *go bowling*. I've got my own ball!

1 I t ake p hotos . I've got some amazing pictures of the lake near our house.

2 We p lay b oard games. We're very good at chess.

3 I r ead c omics . I've got a *Spiderman* from 1991!

4 My parents w atch v ideos . They love romantic comedies.

5 I d o c rafts . I love making things.

5 ★★★ Complete the quiz.

1 You can see this in the Niagara River in the USA or the Iguazu River in Argentina.

waterfall

2 A big one in Spain is in Murcia and is 170km^2.

lake

3 These people build houses.

construction workers

4 This type of transport used horses in the past but now it uses electricity.

tram

5 This type of transport is useful for travelling on water.

ferry

6 This is a small, light computer.

netbook

be and *have got*: present simple

1 ★ **Write A (affirmative), N (negative) or I (interrogative).**

Have you got an MP3 player? I

1 Are your parents tall? I
2 My grandparents haven't got a car. N
3 Eve's really into sport. A
4 Have we got an exam today? I
5 I've got two sisters. A
6 Simon and Nick aren't brothers. N

2 ★★ **Complete the text. Use the affirmative (✓) or negative (✗) of *be* or *have got*.**

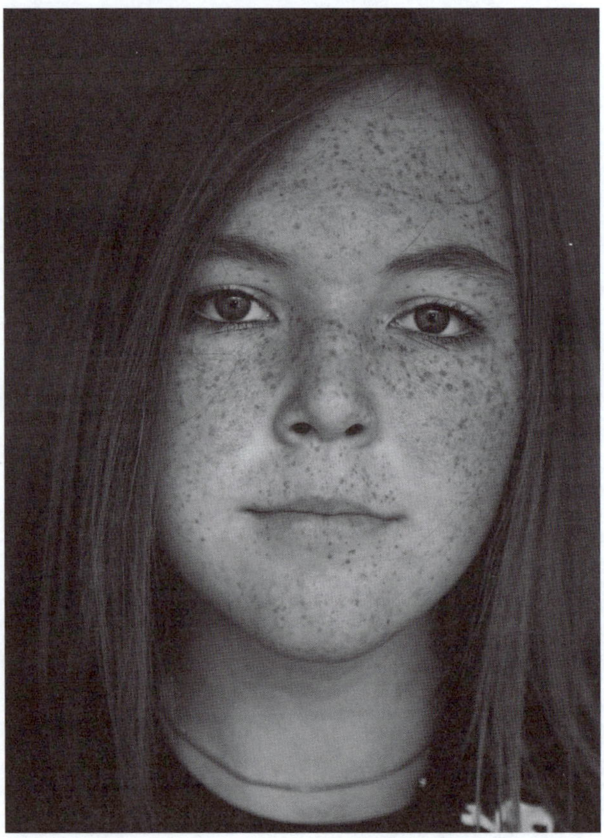

My name's Chris. I'm (✓) fifteen years old. I haven't got (1 ✗) a brother or a sister but we 've got (2 ✓) two dogs. We live in the UK but my mum isn't (3 ✗) British. She 's (4 ✓) Spanish. My parents have got (5 ✓) dark hair but my hair isn't (6 ✗) dark. It 's (7 ✓) red! I 've got (8 ✓) freckles too!

3 ★★ **Complete the questions. Use *be* and *have got*. Then write short answers. Use the text in exercise 2.**

Is the girl's name Alex?
No, it isn't.

1 Has she got a brother?
No, she hasn't.
2 Have her parents got a daughter?
Yes, they have.
3 Are her pets dogs?
Yes, they are.
4 Is her mum British?
No, she isn't.
5 Have her parents got dark hair?
Yes, they have.
6 Has she got freckles?
Yes, she has.

4 ★★★ **Write the questions. Then write true answers. Use *be* and *have got*.**

you fifteen years old?
Are you fifteen years old?
Yes, I am. **or** No, I'm not. I'm fourteen years old.

you / a brother?
Have you got a brother?
Yes, I have. I've got two brothers. **or** No, I haven't. I've got a sister.

1 you / a best friend?
Have you got a best friend?
Students' answers
2 you in a band?
Are you in a band?
3 your mum / a job?
Has your mum got a job?
4 your parents into films?
Are your parents into films?
5 you and your friends / bikes?
Have you and your friends got bikes?

Grammar Bank pages 63–65

can / can't

5 ★ **Put the sentences in the correct order.**

sing / can't / My / dad.
My dad can't sing.

1 can / My sister / the guitar / play.
My sister can play the guitar.

2 can't / I / a car / drive.
I can't drive a car.

3 English / your parents / speak / Can / ?
Can your parents speak English?

4 use / can't / My grandma / the Internet.
My grandma can't use the Internet.

6 ★★ **Correct the mistakes.**

My cousin can **runs** very fast.
My cousin can run very fast.

1 **You can** play basketball?
Can you play basketball?

2 I can't **to understand** this exercise.
I can't understand this exercise.

3 My parents **not can** dance.
My parents can't dance.

4 I **cant'** ski.
I can't ski.

5 Can **skateboard your brother**?
Can your brother skateboard?

6 My dogs **cans** swim.
My dogs can swim.

7 ★★★ **Write questions. Use *can* and a verb. Then write true answers.**

you / sports well?
Can you play sports well?
No, I can't. **or** *Yes, I can. I can play football very well.*

1 you / a car?
Students' answers
______

2 your dad / another language?
______
______

3 your mum / a musical instrument?
______
______

Present continuous

8 ★ **Complete the sentences. Use the present continuous of the verbs in brackets.**

I'm not doing my homework today. (not do)

1 Are Simon and Lucy listening? (listen)

2 The cat isn't sleeping. (not sleep)

3 Look! Your dad 's dancing. (dance)

4 Why 's she running? (run)

9 ★★ **Complete the phone conversation. Use the affirmative, negative or interrogative present continuous of the verbs in the box.**

~~do~~ enjoy go have make
not go not stay show watch

Gav Hi, Mel. What *are* you *doing*?
Mel I **(1)** 'm watching a music programme on TV.
Gav Me too. **(2)** Are you enjoying it?
Mel Yes, I am. They **(3)** 're showing the new Black Eyed Peas video next.
Gav Really? And what are you up to later?
Mel I **(4)** 'm not going out. My dad **(5)** 's making pizza.
Gav I **(6)** 'm having pizza too! But we **(7)** 're not staying at home. We **(8)** 're going to a restaurant.

10 ★★★ **Write true answers.**

Is your mum going out on Saturday?
No, she isn't. She's staying at home.
or
Yes, she is. She's going to a football match.

1 Are you going out at the weekend?
Students' answers

2 Is your mum making dinner?
______

3 Are you walking to school tomorrow?
______

4 Is your class doing an exam next week?
______

Meeting people

1 ★ **Complete the dialogue. Use the words in the box.**

Are you keen on ~~How about you~~ Me too Really What about you

Tia	Hi, my name's Tia. What's your name?
Joe	I'm Joe.
Tia	Which bus are you waiting for?
Joe	The number 76. How about you?
Tia	I'm waiting for the bus to the cinema. I'm watching a film this afternoon.
Joe	**(1)** Really ? That's interesting. **(2)** Are you keen on films?
Tia	Yes, I am. **(3)** What about you ?
Joe	Yes. I love science fiction films.
Tia	**(4)** Me too . Maybe we can watch a film some time. Give me your mobile number. I'll text you.
Joe	OK!

2 ★★ **Are the questions true or false? Write T or F.**

Tia doesn't know Joe. T

1 Tia is waiting for the number 76 bus. F
2 Joe is going to the cinema. F
3 Joe is into science fiction films. T
4 Tia doesn't enjoy science fiction films. F
5 Tia gives Joe her mobile phone number. F

3 ★★ **Answer the questions.**

What's the girl's name?
Her name's Tia.

1 What the boy's name?
His name's Joe.

2 Which bus is the boy waiting for?
The number 76.

3 Where is the girl going?
To the cinema.

4 When is she watching a film?
This afternoon.

5 Is Joe keen on films?
Yes, he is.

6 What type of films does Joe love?
Science fiction films.

4 ★★★ **In your notebook, write a dialogue like the dialogue in exercise 1. Use the guide below.**

Student A	Student B
Introduce yourself. Ask B's name.	
	Answer.
Ask which tram B is waiting for.	
	Reply. Ask A the same question.
Reply. Say where you are going and why.	
	Reply. Ask about interests.
Reply. Ask B the same question.	
	Reply.
Make a suggestion. Ask for B's mobile number.	
	Reply.

1 Relax!

Vocabulary

Leisure activities

1 ★ Circle the leisure activities. Match the words and the photos.

N	P	P	K	L	L	T	A	A
I	G	H	O	V	B	I	S	A
R	C	O	O	K	I	N	G	M
S	R	T	M	U	S	I	C	U
S	D	O	S	F	A	K	H	S
M	A	G	A	Z	I	N	E	S
Q	N	R	F	I	X	N	S	P
G	C	A	N	A	H	J	S	R
V	I	P	V	N	Q	D	V	G
S	N	H	M	F	S	N	V	R
D	G	Y	W	X	Q	C	G	Z

music

3 dancing

1 chess

4 magazines

2 cooking

5 photography

2 ★★ Complete the sentences. Use the words in the box.

computer games cycling drawing fashion films magazines ~~sport~~ the Internet

1 I'm very keen on sport, for example football. I'm also quite interested in cycling but I haven't got a very good bike.

2 My cousin's mad about computers. She uses the Internet a lot and she also plays a lot of computer games with her friends.

3 My sister has got a lot of clothes. She's really into fashion. She also enjoys drawing so she designs T-shirts.

4 I'm a big fan of films. I love going to the cinema and I read a lot of magazines about actors too.

3 ★★★ Complete true sentences about leisure activities.

I'm a big fan of horror films.

1 My best friend's really into Students' answers ______.

2 My classmates are mad ______.

3 I'm not really into ______.

4 My English teacher's keen ______.

5 My parents are quite interested ______.

6 My friends are quite keen ______.

Present simple

1 ★ **Choose the correct options.**

I (love) / **loves** cooking.

1 My cousin doesn't (do) / **does** sport.
2 (Do) / **Does** your grandparents use a computer?
3 My sisters (read) / **reads** a lot of magazines.
4 Do you go cycling a lot? Yes, we (do) / **does**.
5 My best friend **don't** / (doesn't) play chess.
6 What does she (eat) / **eats** for breakfast?

2 ★★ **Complete the sentences. Use the present simple of the verbs in the box.**

hate	not do	~~not like~~	prefer

1 **Paul** My dad isn't really into sport. He *doesn't like* watching sport. He really hates football. He doesn't do any exercise. He prefers watching films.

listen to	look at	not play	send

2 Jenny and her sister are mad about computers but they don't play computer games. They look at websites, watch TV and listen to music on the Internet. Jenny sends a lot of emails every day.

buy	cycle	not use	wash

3 **Eve** My little brother's mad about cycling. He cycles to school every day and he buys new things for his bike when he's got money. He washes his bike every Saturday and he doesn't use his bike when it's raining.

3 ★★★ **Write questions about the people and the activities in the box. Then write true answers.**

People
~~you~~ you and your friends your best friend your dad your English teacher

Activities
buy music on the Internet cook for your parents cycle to work or school do any exercise ~~play chess~~

Do you play chess?
Yes, I do. I play chess every Friday.

1 Students' answers
2
3
4

Adverbs of frequency

4 ★ **Rewrite the sentences. Put the adverbs of frequency in the correct positions.**

It snows in December. (usually)
It usually snows in December.

1 My best friend's late. (always)
My best friend's always late.
2 My dad goes swimming in the morning. (often)
My dad often goes swimming in the morning.
3 My parents are out on Sunday nights. (never)
My parents are never out on Sunday nights.
4 I'm at home on Saturdays. (hardly ever)
I'm hardly ever at home on Saturdays.
5 My cousin and I play chess on the Internet. (sometimes)
My cousin and I sometimes play chess on the Internet.

Grammar Bank pages 66–67

5 ★★ **Study the table. Complete the sentences.**

	Harry	Bess
wash the car	sometimes	often
study on Friday nights	hardly ever	hardly ever
be out on Saturday nights	usually	always
cook dinner	often	sometimes
be in bed before 11 p.m.	never	never

Harry *sometimes washes* the car.

1 Bess often washes the car.
2 Harry and Bess hardly ever study on Friday nights.
3 Harry is usually out on Saturday nights.
4 Bess sometimes cooks dinner.
5 Harry and Bess are never in bed before 11 p.m.

6 ★★★ **Write true sentences. Use adverbs of frequency.**

My dad *hardly ever washes the car* (wash the car).

1 I Students' answers (be bored).
2 The weather ______ (be good) in my town.
3 I ______ (play computer games).
4 My teacher ______ (be late).

Present tense contrast

7 ★ **Choose the correct options.**

My cousin **often plays** / **'s often playing** basketball with his friends.

1 My grandmother and I **talk** / **are talking** on the phone every week.
2 I **usually sit** / **'m usually sitting** in this chair.
3 Look at Mr Parks. He **talks** / **'s talking** to your parents.
4 **Do you know** / **Are you knowing** Alan?
5 **You sit** / **You're sitting** on my book. Can I have it?

8 ★★ **Complete the sentences. Use the present simple or present continuous of the verbs in brackets.**

Lauren	*I'm trying* (try) to do my homework but it's difficult and I need (**1** need) some help. What are you doing (**2** do)?
Karen	We 're watching (**3** watch) a film but I 'm writing (**4** write) a few emails too.
Lauren	I hardly ever watch (**5** watch) films on Sunday night …
Karen	… because you never do (**6** do) your homework before then!
Lauren	You're right! ☺ Now, I 'm (**7** be) hungry …
Karen	I 'm eating (**8** eat) a nice bar of chocolate. Mmmmm. Do you want (**9** want) some?
Lauren	Ha ha!

9 ★★★ **Complete the sentences. Use the present simple or present continuous.**

'What *are* you *eating*?'
'A sandwich.'

1 'Goodnight. We 're going to bed.'
2 'Does your dad sometimes smoke?'
'No, he hates cigarettes.'
3 'You don't look very interested. Are you listening to me?'
'Yes, I am!'
4 'Buenos días!'
'Sorry. I don't speak Spanish.'
5 'Look! The dog's thirsty. She needs a drink.'

Reading

1 **What are your friends' hobbies? Who has got an interesting hobby?**

Ask and answer

You ask, everybody answers!

What's an interesting hobby?

I enjoy my hobbies. I play basketball. I use the Internet – I often visit chat rooms and I love finding out facts. But I'm sometimes still bored! I need another hobby – something unusual. Any ideas?

Joe 10:17

BEST ANSWER

I've got the perfect hobby for you. I'm doing it right now! I answer questions on the Internet. I usually answer about five questions every day. It's really interesting and I learn a lot.

Adam 11:49

My friends and I often watch TV programmes together but we never do it in the same house. We watch TV at our own houses and we send texts to each other while we watch. It makes TV a lot more fun!

Jen 13:12

I like finding shapes in clouds and stars. I often lie in the garden and look at the sky. It's amazing what you can see.

Stephen 17:02

I make presents. It's a fantastic hobby – I'm never bored. At the moment I'm making a chair for my dad's birthday. I found it in the street and I'm painting it.

Ellie 19:46

2 ★ **Read the text. Tick (✓) the main topic.**

a) Cheap hobbies
b) Unusual hobbies ✓
c) Computer hobbies

3 ★★ **Answer the questions.**

Whose hobby uses mobile phones? Jen

1 Whose hobby uses old things? Ellie
2 Whose hobbies use computers? Joe and Adam
3 Whose hobby uses nothing? Stephen

4 ★★ **Are these sentences true or false? Write T or F.**

Joe isn't into sports. F

1 Joe is never bored. F
2 Adam often uses the Internet. T
3 Adam usually asks about five questions every day. F
4 Jen watches TV at her friends' houses. F
5 Jen and her friends like the same TV programmes. T
6 Stephen can only do his hobby during the daytime. F
7 Ellie doesn't think her hobby's interesting. F
8 Ellie bought a chair for her dad's birthday. F

5 ★★★ **Answer the questions.**

What hobbies has Joe got?

He plays basketball and he uses the Internet. He visits chat rooms and finds out facts.

1 What's Adam's hobby and how often does he do it?
He answers questions on the Internet every day.

2 Why does Jen think her way of watching TV is better?
It makes watching TV a lot more fun.

3 Where does Stephen do his hobby?
He does his hobby in the garden.

4 Where did Ellie get the chair?
She found it in the street.

5 What's Ellie doing to her dad's present at the moment?
She's painting it.

Noun endings

1 ★ **Complete the words. Use *-ity*, *-ment* or *-ion*.**

quality
1 react ion
2 argu ment
3 collect ion
4 possibil ity

2 ★★ **Complete the sentences. Use the words in exercise 1.**

I took this photo on my mobile phone so it isn't very good *quality*.
1 Can you hear that? It's Josie. She's having an argument with her brother.
2 I told my teacher about the problem. Her reaction was great.
3 Macie has got a great collection of celebrity autographs.
4 There's a possibility of snow later. I heard it on the radio.

3 ★★★ **Complete the sentences.**

I want to do a creative *activity* for a hobby – like art or photography.
1 I had a bad argument with my parents last night. They're really angry with me.
2 Have you seen Tom's collection of football shirts? He's got about fifty!
3 This CD's really bad quality. Did you copy it on your computer?
4 The economic situation is very bad at the moment. Many people haven't got jobs.

Verb + noun collocation

4 ★ **Choose the correct options.**

visit / meet / take chat rooms
1 **do / send / have** texts
2 **meet / play / go** friends
3 **have / do / go** jogging
4 **have / go / take** a meal out
5 **take / do / play** photos

5 ★★ **Complete the sentences. Use the verbs and nouns in the box.**

Verbs
go have meet sends ~~takes~~
Nouns
a meal out friends jogging ~~photos~~ texts

My aunt *takes photos* for a fashion magazine. It's an amazing job.
1 I often meet friends at the shopping centre on Saturday mornings.
2 We go jogging in the park. I like running and listening to my MP3 player.
3 Dad can't understand mobile phones. He never sends texts.
4 My parents usually have a meal out on Saturdays. They love Spanish food.

6 ★★★ **Read what the people say. Write sentences.**

'The classes are at the sports centre. I'm the only boy there but it really helps me keep fit.'
Mark *does aerobics*.
1 'I usually run about three kilometres. I'd like to do a marathon one day.'
Sally goes jogging.
2 'I really enjoy talking to new people on the Internet and I have friends all over the world.'
Raúl visits chat rooms.
3 'I'm very tall, so it's my favourite sport.'
Jake plays basketball.

4 'I've got a very good camera on my phone.'
Ellen takes photos.

Making arrangements

1 ★ **Put the sentences in the correct order.**

Lucy Fine, thanks. 2
Lucy I'd love to. Thanks! 6
Lucy Not really. Why? 4
Lucy Great! See you there! 8
Matt Have you got any plans for Sunday? 3
Matt Hi, Lucy. How are you? 1
Matt I'm having a party. Do you want to come? 5
Matt We're meeting at the sports centre at six o'clock. 7

2 ★★ **Answer the questions.**

What's Lucy doing on Sunday?
She hasn't got any plans.

1 What does Matt invite Lucy to?
He invites her to come to a party.

2 Where is it happening?
At the sports centre.

3 What time is it happening?
At six o'clock.

4 Can Lucy go?
Yes, she can.

3 ★★★ **Write a dialogue in your notebook like the dialogue in exercise 1. Use the ideas in the box.**

go jogging Friday night about 7:30 p.m. in the park

Dictation

4 ★★ 4.02 **Listen. Listen again and write the sentences in your notebook.**

Personal profile

1 ★ **Match the sentences and the topics.**

1 Personal details: a), d)
2 School: b)
3 Hobbies and interests: c), e)

a) I live with my mum and two cats.
b) My favourite subject's English.
c) I play chess with my best friend, David.
d) My birthday's next week.
e) I've got about 5,000 MP3 songs.

2 ★★ **Cross out the sentences that do not match.**

My sister's mad about fashion. She buys clothes every weekend. ~~She's really into keep fit.~~ She also designs clothes.

1 My dad hates computers. He thinks the Internet's boring. He can't send emails. ~~I love playing chess on my computer.~~

2 Jamie's dad is very clever. He knows everything about computers. ~~He's mad about cycling.~~ He's got his own website.

3 My best friend's really into music. ~~She hasn't got many DVDs.~~ She always carries her MP3 player. She plays the guitar and the piano.

3 ★★★ **Complete the profile.**

Name: *Oliver* ***Age:*** *14*
Lives: *Oxford, with parents and two sisters*
School: *Park Secondary* ***Year:*** *10*
Best subject: *maths*
Worst subject: *French*
Free time: *collects comics – has got over 500, buys them on the Internet*

My name's Oliver. I'm (**1**) fourteen and I live in (**2**) Oxford, (**3**) with my parents and my two sisters.

I'm a student at (**4**) Park Secondary. I'm in Year (**5**) 10. My favourite (**6**) subject is maths and my worst (**7**) subject is French.

In my free time I (**8**) collect comics. I've got (**9**) over 500. I (**10**) buy them on the Internet.

Writing Builder page 102

2 Happy endings?

Vocabulary

Describing feelings

1 ★ **Look at the picture stories. Complete the words.**

1 surprised
2 _e_ x c _i_ t _e_ d
3 d _i_ s _a_ p p _o_ _i_ n t _e_ d

4 l _o_ n _e_ l y
5 d _e_ l _i_ g h t _e_ d
6 r _e_ l _a_ x _e_ d

2 ★★ **How are these people feeling? Complete the crossword.**

1 When you can't understand something
2 Very tired
3 When something happens that you didn't expect
4 Unhappy
5 Angry
6 A bit angry or bored because of something that you have experienced for too long
7 A bit annoyed
8 Frightened

1 C	O	N	F	U	S	2 E	D	
						X		
	3 S			4 U		H		
	U			P		A		
5 C	R	O	S	S		U		6 F
	P			E		S		E
7 I	R	R	I	T	A	T	E	D
	I					E		U
	8 S	C	A	R	E	D		P
	E							
	D							

3 ★★★ **Write true answers.**

When do you feel relaxed?
I feel relaxed after school on Friday afternoons.

1 When do you feel jealous?
Students' answers

2 When do you feel scared?

3 When do you feel embarrassed?

4 When do you feel nervous?

Past simple

1 ★ **Complete the sentences. Use the past simple of the verbs in brackets.**

I *arrived* (arrive) at school early this morning.

1 They danced (dance) all night at the party.
2 My mum did (do) aerobics last night.
3 We had (have) a meal out on Friday.
4 Mr Tate said (say) my homework was very good.
5 It rained (rain) all day yesterday.
6 I chatted (chat) to an English boy on holiday.
7 Seb and I went (go) cycling on Saturday.
8 You found (find) my coat!
9 I felt (feel) exhausted this morning.

2 ★ **Choose the correct options.**

Alex Hi, Joe.
Joe Hi, Alex. Did you and your parents **have** / **had** a nice meal last night?
Alex Yes, we did. How (1) **you knew** / **did you know** about it?
Joe Let me guess. You (2) **have** / **had** chicken but you didn't (3) **have** / **had** salad.
Alex Yes!
Joe Your mum (4) **talked** / **talks** about buying a new car.
Alex Yes! Did you (5) **go** / **went** to the same restaurant?
Joe No, I (6) **don't** / **didn't**. (7) **Do** / **Did** you have your mobile phone in your pocket last night?
Alex Yes, I did. Oh no! Did I phone you?
Joe Yes, you (8) **did** / **phoned**. I (9) **hear** / **heard** everything.
Alex Well, we (10) **not** / **didn't** talk about anything interesting.
Joe I know! I was really disappointed!

3 ★★ **Complete the story. Use the past simple of the verbs in the boxes.**

~~meet~~ not tell say want watch

At the weekend, my dad and I **met** my friend at the cinema. My dad (**1**) wanted to see the new James Bond film. He loves action films and he (**2**) watched lots of Bond films when he was young. He (**3**) said the reviews of the new film were fantastic. My friend and I prefer romantic comedies but we (**4**) didn't tell my dad.

buy feel hate not have not want wait

The queue was very long and we (**5**) waited for an hour. When we got to the ticket office, Dad was really excited. Then the woman said they (**6**) didn't have any more tickets! We all (**7**) felt really disappointed but we (**8**) didn't want to go home. So we (**9**) bought tickets to see a romantic comedy. Dad (**10**) hated it, of course, but we really enjoyed it!

4 ★★ **Rewrite these sentences. Use the past simple.**

They leave at six o'clock.
They left at six o'clock.

1 I don't cycle to school.
I didn't cycle to school.

2 Do you cook?
Yes, I do.
Did you cook?
Yes, I did.

3 What time do you get up?
I get up at about 7:30 a.m.
What time did you get up?
I got up at about 7:30 a.m.

4 That boy lives in my street.
That boy lived in my street.

5 Does your mum study English?
No, she doesn't.
Did your mum study English?
No, she didn't.

Grammar Bank pages 68–69

5 ★★★ **Write questions and answers. Use the information in the chart.**

Last Saturday	Maria	Raúl and Ines
play a game	✓ (football)	(1) ✓ (basketball)
go away	(2) ✓ (to the beach)	(3) ✗
buy a DVD	(4) ✗	(5) ✓ (a science fiction film)
lose something important	(6) ✓ (mobile phone)	(7) ✗

Did Maria play a game last Saturday?
Yes, she did. She played football.

1 Did Raúl and Ines play a game last Saturday?
Yes, they did. They played basketball.

2 Did Maria go away last Saturday?
Yes, she did. She went to the beach.

3 Did Raúl and Ines go away last Saturday?
No, they didn't.

4 Did Maria buy a DVD last Saturday?
No, she didn't.

5 Did Raúl and Ines buy a DVD last Saturday?
Yes, they did. They bought a science fiction film.

6 Did Maria lose something important last Saturday?
Yes, she did. She lost her mobile phone.

7 Did Raúl and Ines lose something important last Saturday?
No, they didn't.

Past simple of *be*: *was* / *were*

6 ★ **Choose the correct options.**

My brother and I **was** / **(were)** late for school this morning.

1 **Was** / **(Were)** your mum and dad happy with your exam results? Yes, they were.

2 The weather **(wasn't)** / **weren't** good on my birthday.

3 **She was** / **(Was she)** surprised about the party? Yes, she was.

4 **Was I** / **(I was)** exhausted after the race.

7 ★★ **Make the sentences affirmative (✓), negative (✗) or interrogative (?). Use the past simple of *be*.**

I'm nervous. ✗
I wasn't nervous.

1 Are you hot? ✓
You were hot.

2 Sal's at school today. ?
Was Sal at school today?

3 Is your homework in your bag? ✗
Your homework wasn't in your bag.

4 Vic isn't at home. ?
Was Vic at home?

5 Our last lesson isn't maths. ✓
Our last lesson was maths.

6 They're at home all weekend. ✗
They weren't at home all weekend.

8 ★★★ **Complete the conversation. Use the correct forms of *was* / *were*.**

Jen I was in an exam all afternoon.
Mia How (1) was it?
Jen It (2) wasn't easy. The questions (3) were really confusing. I didn't understand some of them.
Mia (4) Were the other students worried?
Jen No, they (5) weren't. But Jacob thought it (6) was impossible. He (7) wasn't very happy after the exam. He felt quite upset.

1 **Look at the photo. How does the girl feel?**

Last week we asked you for a true story with a happy ending.

Letter of the week

Last year I started going out with this boy at my school, Adam. It was cool. We were really into the same things. Then, on my birthday, he was really strange. When I phoned him, he said he was busy. We had an argument about it and I felt really confused. Why didn't he want to see me on my birthday?

I decided to go to my best friend Emma's house and talk to her. Emma's back door's always open. As I wandered into her kitchen, I heard a boy's voice – Adam's! Suddenly I felt really jealous! I ran into the living room quickly. I was really upset and I shouted at them both. They didn't say anything. Then Adam moved away from Emma and I could see behind them.... There was a poster with 'Happy Birthday Jess!' on it. My family and friends were all in Emma's living room. It was a surprise birthday party!

A happy ending, but I was really embarrassed!

Jess Halsey, Brighton, UK

2 ★ **Read the text. Match the names in the box and the people.**

Adam   Emma   ~~Jess~~

The person telling the story. Jess

1 The storyteller's boyfriend. Adam

2 The storyteller's best friend. Emma

3 ★★ **Answer the questions.**

When did Jess argue with her boyfriend?
On her birthday.

1 How did Jess feel after the argument?
Confused.

2 Whose house did she go to?
Emma's house.

3 Which room did Jess walk into first?
The kitchen.

4 What did she hear?
Adam's voice.

5 How did she feel when she shouted at them?
Upset.

6 What was on the poster?
Happy Birthday Jess!

7 Who was in Emma's living room?
Jess's family and friends.

4 ★★★ **Complete the summary.**

It was Jess's birthday.

1 She had an argument with her boyfriend.

2 She went to her friend Emma's house.

3 Her boyfriend, Adam, was there.

4 She felt upset so she shouted at Emma and Adam.

5 It was a surprise birthday party.

6 She felt happy but embarrassed.

Verbs of movement

1 ★ **Look at the picture. Match the verbs and the names.**

fall — b) the books
1 climb — a) the cat
2 wander — d) Dad
3 dive — c) the fish

2 ★★ **Complete the sentences. Use the verbs in the box.**

climb crawl dive fall jump ~~run~~ walk

Don't *run* near the swimming pool. It's very dangerous.

1 You can swim but you can't *dive* here. The water isn't very deep.
2 Don't *jump* on the bed. I'm scared that it will break.
3 My brother's a baby so he can *crawl* but he can't *walk*.
4 Please don't *climb* the trees. You might *fall* and hurt yourself.

3 ★★★ **Look at the picture in exercise 1. Say what the people are doing.**

Sue and Ella are *running*.

1 Mum's *walking*.
2 Josh is *crawling*.
3 Sam's *jumping*.

Prepositions of movement

4 ★ **Choose the correct options.**

I walked **past** / **off** your house last night.

1 The cat's climbing **into** / **onto** the table.
2 We walked **onto** / **along** the beach for two kilometres.
3 Don't walk **towards** / **away from** me. I'm talking to you!
4 We paid and got **off** / **out of** the taxi.

5 ★★ **Complete the sentences. Use the words in the box and the picture in exercise 1.**

away from into off ~~round~~ towards

Dad's wandering *round* the room.

1 Mum's walking *towards* Dad.
2 The books are falling *off* the shelf.
3 Sue's running *away from* Ella.
4 The fish is diving *into* the fishbowl.

6 ★★★ **Complete true sentences. Use prepositions and verbs of movement.**

On the way home, I always *walk past the shop*.

1 Every day, I *Students' answers* ________________.
2 When I see a friend, I ________________.
3 I can ________________.

On the phone

1 ★ **Put the sentences in the correct order.**

Ollie Yes, it was great. 5
Kelly It wasn't great. 8
Ollie Hello. 1
Ollie I met some friends on Saturday night and we had a meal out. What about you? How was your weekend? 7
Kelly Fine thanks. Did you have a good weekend? 4
Kelly I fell off a chair. And I couldn't go jogging, because I hurt my ankle. 10
Ollie Why was that? 9
Ollie Fine. And you? 3
Ollie Oh, dear! Poor you! 11
Kelly Hi, Ollie. This is Kelly. How are you? 2
Kelly What did you do? 6

2 ★★ **Answer the questions.**

Who's phoning who?
Kelly's phoning Ollie.

1 How was Ollie's weekend?
It was great.

2 Why?
He met some friends and they had a meal out.

3 How was Kelly's weekend?
It wasn't great.

4 Why?
She fell off a chair and she hurt her ankle. She couldn't go jogging.

3 ★★★ **Write a dialogue in your notebook like the dialogue in exercise 1. Use the ideas in the box.**

You're phoning your friend Ana.
She was in a swimming competition on Sunday.
She won. You played a football match.
Your team lost.

Dictation

4 ★★ 4.03 **Listen. Listen again and write the sentences in your notebook.**

Sequencing words

1 ★ **Choose the correct options.**

We had lunch in the café. **Later** / **When** we met some friends.

1 **Then** / **Before** I went out, I wrote a note to my parents.
2 I got up **when** / **finally** the phone rang.
3 **First of all** / **Before** he said 'sorry'. **Finally** / **Then** he bought me flowers.
4 **Later** / **After** I finished my homework, I put my books in my bag.

2 ★★ **Complete the sentences. Use the words in the box.**

after before finally ~~first of all~~ when

My mum stays very fit. First of all, she goes jogging every morning. Then, she often does aerobics in the afternoons.

1 After three hours' driving, we finally arrived home.
2 When you knocked on the door, I was in the bath. Sorry.
3 I left the house after it started raining so I got wet!
4 My twin brother started walking two months before me. He's always first at everything!

3 ★★★ **Complete the account of events. Use your own ideas.**

When Katy arrived home yesterday, she felt exhausted.

1 First of all, she Students' answers ______.
2 Next, she ______.
3 After her sandwich, she ______.
4 Then suddenly ______.
5 Before Katy picked up the phone, she ______.

It was her best friend, Martha.

Writing Builder page 103

3 Right or wrong?

Vocabulary

Crime

1 ★ **Complete the words. Match the words and the pictures.**

a r s o n a)

1 m u r d e r b)

2 t h e f t f)

3 d r u g d e a l i n g c)

4 h a c k i n g e)

5 s p e e d i n g d)

a)

d)

b)

e)

c)

f)

2 ★★ **Answer the questions. Use the words in the box.**

~~arson~~ burglary hacking joyriding joyriding shoplifting speeding theft vandalism

Which crime involves fire? *arson*

1 Which crime uses computers? hacking

2 Which crime often uses paint? vandalism

3 Which crimes use cars? joyriding, speeding

4 Which crimes are about stealing things? burglary, joyriding, shoplifting, theft

3 ★★★ **Complete the sentences about crimes.**

Speeding's a serious problem in my street. Cars often drive down it at over 60 kilometres an hour!

1 The police think the wife killed her husband. They arrested her for murder.

2 There was a burglary in our street last night. They took TVs and computers.

3 They arrested the girl for shoplifting. She had some new trousers in her bag.

4 There was some vandalism after the concert. Fans painted the band's name on the walls of the stadium.

5 The fire destroyed three houses. Police think it was arson.

6 They arrested the man for hacking. The police took all his computers.

7 They crashed the car but luckily they weren't hurt. The police arrested them for joyriding.

Past continuous

1 ★ **Complete the interview. Use the past continuous forms of the verbs in brackets.**

Police officer	Tell me everything that you did yesterday. What were you doing at 7 a.m.?
Daniel	I *was sleeping* (sleep).
Police officer	And at 11 a.m.?
Daniel	I was having (**1** have) a shower.
Police officer	What were you doing at 1 p.m.?
Daniel	A friend and I were eating (**2** eat) lunch.
Police officer	OK. What were you doing at 4 p.m?
Daniel	I was swimming (**3** swim). Two people saw me.
Police officer	What were you doing at 8 p.m.?
Daniel	A neighbour and I were talking (**4** talk).
Police officer	Now, at 11 p.m. someone broke into the house. What were you doing then?
Daniel	I wasn't feeling (**5** not feel) well. I was watching (**6** watch) a film at home.

2 ★ **Choose the correct options.**

While we were sleeping, someone (**broke**)/ **was breaking** into the house and took our TV.

1 The woman **didn't listen** / (**wasn't listening**) when the police shouted 'Stop!', so she didn't stop running.

2 I was waiting for a bus when I (**saw**)/ **was seeing** the teenagers steal the car.

3 When you (**broke**)/ **were breaking** your leg, were you being careful?

4 The police arrived while the man **climbed** / (**was climbing**) out of the window.

5 (**Did you hear**)/ **Were you hearing** any noises while you were having dinner?

3 ★★ **Write sentences. Use the past continuous.**

you / listen / to me?
Were you listening to me?

1 I / wait / for you near the cinema.
I was waiting for you near the cinema.

2 Mark and Silvia / not argue.
Mark and Silvia weren't arguing.

3 the students / revise / for their exams?
Were the students revising for their exams?

4 Steve and I / swim on Saturday morning.
Steve and I were swimming on Saturday morning.

5 I / not wear / a jacket yesterday.
I wasn't wearing a jacket yesterday.

6 your brother / chat / to my sister?
Was your brother chatting to my sister?

4 ★★ **Complete the sentences. Use the past simple or the past continuous of the verbs in the box.**

~~crawl~~	leave	not carry	put	run

The police caught the boys while they *were crawling* under the fence.

1 When I walked past the shop, three men were running out of it.

2 Was it raining when you left your house this morning?

3 You weren't carrying an umbrella when you arrived.

4 While I was talking to my friend, she put her glasses in her bag.

Grammar Bank pages 70–71

5 ★★★ **Complete Zack's story. Use the past simple or the past continuous of the verbs in the boxes.**

hear look run say shout stop ~~walk~~

I was walking home from school when I (**1**) heard a woman shout.

'That's one of them!' she said.

I (**2**) looked up quickly. Two women looked very annoyed and a man (**3**) was running towards me! I was scared so I ran. While I was trying to escape, I could hear the man behind me. He (**4**) was shouting loudly.

'Stop!' he (**5**) was saying. 'Police!' Police? I (**6**) stopped immediately.

clean not carry not know not wear speak take

'I (**7**) didn't know you were a police officer,' I said. The man (**8**) wasn't wearing a uniform. He (**9**) took me back to the shop. The women (**10**) were cleaning some paint off the wall.

'Vandalism's a serious crime,' the police officer said. While I was explaining that I was innocent, one of the women (**11**) spoke.

'I'm sorry,' she said. 'I wasn't looking carefully. This isn't one of the boys. They (**12**) weren't carrying school bags.'

6 ★★★ **Read Zack's story again. Complete the questions.**

Where was Zack going?
Home.

1 What was the man shouting?
'Stop! Police!'

2 Was he wearing a uniform?
No, he wasn't.

3 Were the boys carrying school bags?
No, they weren't.

Adverbs

7 ★ **Write *adverb* or *adjective* or *both* next to each word.**

good *adjective*
1 sleepy adjective
2 badly adverb
3 hard both
4 quick adjective
5 late both
6 luckily adverb
7 early both
8 noisy adjective
9 well adverb

8 ★★ **Complete the sentences. Use adverbs from exercise 7.**

My mum speaks English really well. She lived in England for ten years.

1 The party was in the garden. Luckily, the sun was shining.

2 We got to the airport late and missed the plane.

3 I revised very badly and wasn't ready for the exam.

4 Everyone worked hard on the project and the teacher was delighted.

9 ★★★ **Write true sentences. Use adverbs formed from the adjectives in the box.**

bad ~~beautiful~~ good noisy quick

My sister dances beautifully.

1 Students' answers
2 ______
3 ______
4 ______

1 **Look at the photos. What's happening to the boy?**

True stories

When Marion got home after work, she knew something was wrong.

'First of all, I saw the broken window.'

A police officer arrived fifteen minutes later. Marion's jewellery was missing – and about £50. Then, when the police officer was looking at the window, he noticed something strange. The broken glass was *outside* the house.

'If you break a window from the outside, the glass falls inside,' he told her. 'Someone broke this window from *inside* the house.' Marion felt sick.

'We knew Ned was sometimes in trouble – some shoplifting a few years ago. But *burglary* – stealing from his *parents*!'

Marion waited until her son got home.

'Was it you?' she asked him.

Marion didn't need to wait for an answer. She knew immediately. She calmly phoned the police and told them the truth.

Ned got a year in a special prison for young people. His parents' burglary wasn't his first. For three months he was too upset to talk to them. Marion says she and her husband spent every day thinking about her decision. Then, Ned wrote and invited his parents to visit. Now they see him every week and they plan what Ned will do with his life when he's free again.

2 ★ **Read the text. Choose the best title.**

(a) My son burgled my house

b) My first burglary

c) My son steals from shops

3 ★★ **Put the events in the correct order.**

Ned's parents visited him. 7

A police officer came to the house. 3

Ned went to prison. 6

Marion called the police about her son. 5

Ned burgled his parents' house. 1

The police officer told Marion something strange. 4

Marion got home. 2

4 ★★★ **Answer the questions.**

What did Marion see when she got home?
She saw a broken window.

1 What did the police officer notice?
He noticed that the broken glass was outside the house.

2 Why was Ned in trouble a few years ago?
Ned was in trouble for shoplifting a few years ago.

3 What happened when Ned got home?
Marion asked him about the burglary.

4 Why didn't Ned want to talk to his parents?
He was upset because they told the police.

5 How did Ned contact his parents again?
He wrote them a letter.

Adjective endings

1 ★ **Complete the words. Use *-al, -ful, -ous* or *-y*. Match the words and the photos.**

cloudy *a)*

1 power<u>ful</u> <u>e)</u>

2 dirt<u>y</u> <u>d)</u>

3 music<u>al</u> <u>c)</u>

4 danger<u>ous</u> <u>b)</u>

a)

b)

c)

d)

e)

2 ★★ **Complete the crossword. Make adjectives from the nouns.**

1 sun 4 health 6 care

2 nature 5 juice 7 mystery

3 colour

	1 S	U	N	2 N	Y				
				A				3 C	
4 H	E	A	L	T	H	Y		O	
				U				L	
	5 J			R				O	
	U		6 C	A	R	E	F	U	L
	I			L				R	
	C							F	
7 M	Y	S	T	E	R	I	O	U	S
								L	

3 ★★ **Complete the sentences. Use adjectives from exercise 2.**

When I do exercise, I feel really **healthy**.

1 I like your T-shirt. It's really <u>colourful</u>.

2 Be <u>careful</u>! These stairs are dangerous.

3 These oranges are really <u>juicy</u>.

4 You don't need a jacket. It's <u>sunny</u> outside.

5 I don't know anything about Paul – he's very <u>mysterious</u>.

6 I prefer <u>natural</u> drinks, like juice and water, to fizzy drinks.

4 ★★★ **Complete the sentences.**

I love this song. It's very **beautiful**.

1 We have a <u>national</u> holiday on Monday. All my friends are going to the beach.

2 When you were in Hollywood, did you meet anyone <u>famous</u>?

3 This bread's really <u>tasty</u>. Can I have some more?

4 You don't have to do this exercise. It's <u>optional</u>.

5 An earthquake is a <u>natural</u> disaster.

6 The weather can be really <u>rainy</u> in this part of the country. But all the water keeps the plants <u>healthy</u>.

Making suggestions

1 ★ Complete the dialogue. Use the words in the box.

a good idea | did that | ~~don't know what to do~~ | How about reading | What about | why don't you

Ben I'm bored. I *don't know what to do.*
Dad (1) How about reading a book?
Ben No, I (2) did that this afternoon.
Dad Well, (3) why don't you go out for a walk?
Ben No, I'm exhausted.
Dad (4) What about going to bed?
Ben Yeah! That's (5) a good idea ! Good night!

2 ★★ Read the dialogue in exercise 1. Complete the chart.

Dad's suggestion	Ben's reaction
How about *reading a book?*	(1) He did that this afternoon .
(2) Why don't you go out for a walk ?	(3) He's exhausted .
(4) What about going to bed ?	(5) He thinks that's a good idea .

3 ★★★ Write a dialogue in your notebook like the dialogue in exercise 1. Use some of the ideas in the table.

Suggestions	Objections
cook dinner	haven't got any food
take some photos	don't feel like it
go jogging	trainers are wet
do your homework	did it yesterday

Dictation

4 ★★ 4.04 **Listen. Listen again and write the sentences in your notebook.**

Describing a scene

1 ★ Choose the correct options.

I'm not buying him a present **and** / **(or)** going to his party.

1 I was sitting at home **(and)** / **or** thinking about the future.
2 The teacher wasn't smiling **and** / **(or)** joking.
3 They're watching TV **(and)** / **or** having dinner.

2 ★ Cross out the extra words.

I was sitting and ~~I was~~ waiting for you.

1 We were having a sandwich and ~~we were~~ drinking some coffee.
2 They're shouting and ~~they're~~ screaming.

3 ★★ Rewrite the sentences more concisely. Remember that you may have to change *and* to *or*.

We were sitting and we were doing our work.
We were sitting and doing our work.

1 My friends weren't listening and they weren't being careful.
My friends weren't listening or being careful.
2 The rain was warm and it was light.
The rain was warm and light.
3 I wasn't feeling happy and I wasn't relaxed.
I wasn't feeling happy or relaxed.

4 ★★★ Complete the description. Use the notes.

Got home, cloudy, starting to rain
Put key in lock, opened door
Dog wasn't waiting, not jumping at door
Walked into kitchen, saw broken door

When I got home, it *was cloudy and starting to rain.* I put (1) my key in the lock and opened the door . Something was wrong. Our dog (2) wasn't waiting or jumping at the door . I walked (3) into the kitchen and saw the the broken door . Suddenly, I heard a noise.

Writing Builder page 104

4 Home sweet home!

Vocabulary

Household tasks

1 ★ **Choose the correct options. Then match the phrases and the photos.**

(clean) / put / make the floor *c)*

1 do / (put) / clean the rubbish out a)
2 clean / (do) / make the washing f)
3 (do) / clean / make the dusting b)
4 (make) / do / put your bed d)
5 make / put / (do) the cooking e)

a) 

d) 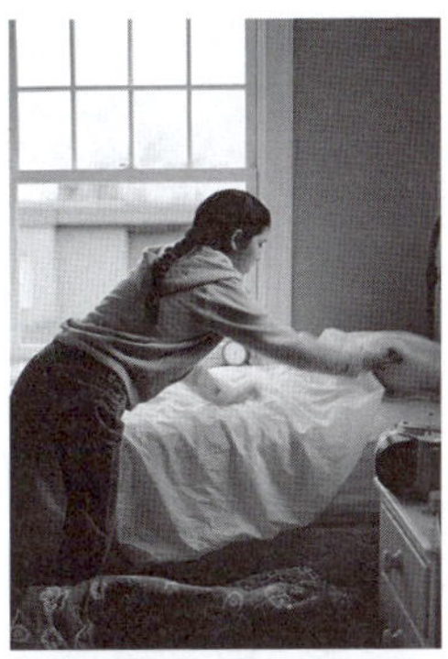

b) 

e) 

c) 

f) 

2 ★★ **Complete the crossword.**

1 Looking after the plants and the grass.
2 You do this when plates are dirty.
3 You do the ironing on an ironing … .
4 You wash clothes in a washing … .
5 Buying food, etc.
6 You do the hoovering with a … .
7 You cook food with a … .
8 You put the … in a dustbin.

										1 G		
										A		
										R		
				2 W		3 B	O	A	R	D		
				A						E		
		4 M		5 S	H	O	P	P	I	N	G	
		A		H						I		
6 V	A	C	U	U	M	7 C	L	E	A	N	E	R
		H		P		O				G		
		I				O						
		N				K						
		E				E						
						8 R	U	B	B	I	S	H

3 ★★★ **Write true sentences about the household tasks you and your family do. Use adverbs of frequency from the box.**

always hardly ever never ~~often~~
sometimes usually

I often tidy up.

1 Students' answers
2 ______
3 ______
4 ______
5 ______

have to

1 ★ **Choose the correct options.**

We **(have to)** / **don't have to** study maths at school. It's compulsory.

1 Tom **has to** / **(doesn't have to)** come home early at the weekend. He can stay out late.
2 My mum **has to** / **(doesn't have to)** do the shopping. My dad does it.
3 Sally and Fred **(have to)** / **don't have to** go to school on Saturdays, but only in the morning.
4 I **(have to)** / **don't have to** go now or I'll miss the last bus home.
5 Rachel **(has to)** / **doesn't have to** revise for her exams. They start next week.

2 ★★ **Read the note. Write sentences. Use *have to*.**

Dear Freddie and Lola,

Tidy your rooms.

1 Make your beds.
2 Freddie, do the washing.
3 Lola, do the hoovering in your room.
4 Wash up.

Only if you have time:

5 Do the shopping.
6 Do the cooking.
7 Freddie: do the dusting in your room.

Have a fun day!
Mum and Dad x

Freddie and Lola have to tidy their rooms.

1 They have to make their beds.
2 Freddie has to do the washing.
3 Lola has to do the hoovering in her room.
4 They have to wash up.
5 They don't have to do the shopping.
6 They don't have to do the cooking.
7 Freddie doesn't have to do the dusting in his room.

3 ★★★ **Complete the sentences. Use the correct forms of *have to* and the verbs in the box.**

be do do do get up ~~help~~ pay put

Teenagers usually have to help with the housework.

1 Young children don't usually have to do the shopping.
2 I can't go out today. I have to do some homework.
3 Ben has to put the rubbish out every day or he doesn't get any pocket money.
4 I'm going now but Maria doesn't have to be home until nine o'clock.
5 Does your dad have to get up early in the morning?
6 You don't have to pay me now. Give me the money later.
7 Do I have to do this exercise?
Yes, you do.

some and any

4 ★ **Choose the correct options.**

Are there **some** / **(any)** puzzles in that magazine?

1 We've got **(some)** / **any** great DVDs.
2 Would you like **(some)** / **any** cheese?
3 There aren't **some** / **(any)** good films on at the cinema.
4 There are **(some)** / **any** plates in the sink.
5 Have you got **some** / **(any)** interesting books?
6 Can we have **(some)** / **any** water, please?
7 I haven't got **some** / **(any)** paper.

Grammar Bank pages 72–73

5 ★★ **Complete the dialogue. Use *some* and *any*.**

Dad We haven't got any milk. Can you get (1) some from the shop, please?
Cassy I haven't got (2) any money. Can you give me (3) some money, please?
Dad OK. There's (4) some money on my desk. Take one euro.
Cassy Is there (5) any juice in the fridge?
Dad No, there isn't.
Cassy And have we got (6) any bread?
Dad No, we haven't.
Cassy So, I have to get (7) some milk, juice and bread ... with one euro.
Dad OK. Take five euros, then!

6 ★★★ **Rewrite the sentences in the affirmative (✓), negative (✗) or interrogative (?).**

There's some rubbish in the bin. **?**
Is there any rubbish in the bin?

1 There are some good programmes on TV. ✗
There aren't any good programmes on TV.

2 We haven't got any butter. **?**
Have we got any butter?

3 There isn't any fruit. ✓
There's some fruit.

4 He'd like some water. **?**
Would he like some water?

5 We've got some sandwiches. **?**
Have we got any sandwiches?

6 They've got some soup. ✗
They haven't got any soup.

7 We haven't got any pasta. ✓
We've got some pasta.

8 There's some cheese in the fridge. **?**
Is there any cheese in the fridge?

much, many, a lot of

7 ★ **Choose the correct options.**

1 How (**much**) / **many** coffee (**is**) / **are** there?
There isn't (**much**) / **many** coffee.

2 How (**many**) / **much** photos **is** / (**are**) there?
There are (**a lot of**) / **much** photos.

3 How **much** / (**many**) cups **is** / (**are**) there?
There aren't **a lot of** / (**many**) cups.

4 How (**much**) / **many** soup (**is**) / **are** there?
There's (**a lot of**) / **much** soup.

8 ★★ **Complete the sentences. Use *much*, *many* or *a lot of*.**

1 There isn't much fruit. There were a lot of bananas and oranges yesterday.

2 Please can you wash up? There aren't many clean dishes.

3 How much money can I borrow?

4 There's a lot of dirty washing in the bathroom. The washing machine's in the kitchen.

5 How much time is there before the train leaves?

6 There weren't many people at the party that I knew. A lot of Adam's friends were there.

9 ★★★ **Complete the questions. Write true answers. Use *much* and *many*.**

How much cheese is there in your fridge?
There isn't much cheese in my fridge.

1 How many English words do you know?
Students' answers

2 How much spare time do you have every day?

3 How many students are there in your school?

4 How much juice do you drink every year?

1 **Have you ever asked a question on the Internet? What was the question?**

Tom
Oxford

My mum says that I have to do more at home – household tasks like washing up. We're having a lot of arguments about this at the moment. I know she's upset. How much does everyone else help at home?

Rick
Aberdeen

To be honest, I do nothing. Yesterday my mum walked into my bedroom and it was so untidy that she thought there were burglars! She doesn't get cross about it, though. She says if I want to live in a dustbin it's my decision. So she says I don't have to do anything!

Sarah
Canterbury

Wow! Lucky you, Rick! My brother and I have to help a lot around the house. We always tidy our rooms and make our beds. We also have to wash up and sometimes I do the washing. If mum or dad don't have time, my brother sometimes has to do the shopping. He can drive.

Ruby
Cornwall

I have to do the usual things and I try to help with the hoovering and the cooking. But if your mum's upset you obviously have to help her more. So stop worrying about what other people are doing and start helping her!

2 ★ **Read the text. Tick the household tasks from the text.**

doing the washing ✓
1 putting the rubbish out __
2 doing the cooking ✓
3 doing the gardening __
4 doing the hoovering ✓
5 tidying up ✓
6 doing the ironing __
7 doing the shopping ✓
8 washing up ✓

3 ★★ **Answer the questions.**

Whose mum isn't happy? *Tom's mum*
1 Whose mum's very relaxed? Rick's mum
2 Who thinks Tom has to help more? Ruby
3 Who can drive? Sarah's brother
4 Who doesn't have to do any housework? Rick
5 Who does a lot of housework? Sarah, Sarah's brother and Ruby

4 ★★★ **Answer the questions.**

Why are Tom and his mum having a lot of arguments?
His mum says that he has to do more at home.
1 How does his mum feel?
She feels upset.
2 Is Rick's mum cross with him?
No, she isn't.
3 Why isn't Rick's mum worried about his room?
She says it's his decision.
4 What does Sarah's brother have to do at home?
He has to tidy his room, make his bed, wash up and do the shopping.
5 What's Ruby's advice to Tom?
He has to help his mum more.

do, have, make

1 ★ **Complete the phrases. Use *do*, *have* or *make*. Match the phrases and the photos.**

make friends a)

1 do the gardening f)

2 have a terrible time c)

3 have a rest e)

4 make a mistake d)

5 do the housework b)

a)

b)

c)

d)

e)

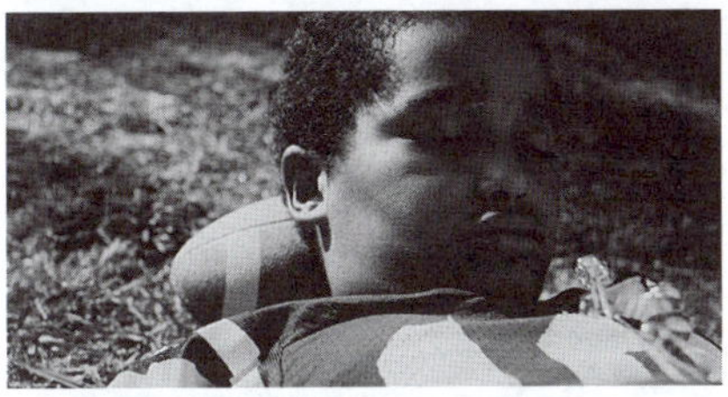

f)

2 ★★ **Complete the sentences. Use the phrases in exercise 1.**

James and I made friends on our first day at school.

1 We had a terrible time on holiday. It rained every day!

2 My dad says I have to do the housework with him on Saturday. I hate cleaning!

3 I made a mistake. Sorry. There isn't much milk.

4 Why don't you have a rest? You're exhausted.

5 My mum does the gardening. She's really into plants.

3 ★★★ **Write phrases under the pictures. Use *do*, *have* or *make*.**

have a drink

3 do the housework

1 make dinner

4 do some work

2 have an argument

5 make a phone call

Invitations

1 ★ **Put the sentences in the correct order.**

Sophie	I'd love to, but I can't. 7
Sophie	At seven o'clock. 3
Sophie	Rob and I are going out for a meal on Saturday evening. Would you like to come? 1
Sophie	Yes. See you on Saturday at seven! 9
Sophie	That's great. 5
David	That's a shame. Maybe another time. 8
David	What time are you going? 2
David	OK. I'm going to the cinema tonight. Would you like to come? 6
David	Yes, I'd love to. 4

2 ★★ **Answer the questions.**

What does Sophie invite David to?
A meal out.

1 Who's going?
Rob and Sophie.

2 What time are they going?
At seven o'clock.

3 What does David invite Sophie to?
The cinema.

4 Does she accept the invitation?
No, she doesn't.

3 ★★★ **Write a dialogue in your notebook like the dialogue in exercise 1. Use the ideas in the table.**

Rachel	Joe
Invitation: watch a football match on TV on Saturday afternoon Time: 2:30 p.m.	Invitation: go cycling Time: this afternoon

Dictation

4 ★★ 4.05 **Listen. Listen again and write the sentences in your notebook.**

Article

1 ★ **Complete the chart. Use the adjectives in the box.**

~~big~~ grey metal new old round Russian small square Turkish white wooden

Size	Age	Shape	Colour	Origin	Material
big	new	round	grey	Russian	metal
small	old	square	white	Turkish	wooden

2 ★★ **Put the words in the correct order. If you need help, use the chart in exercise 1.**

white / washing machine / a / big / old
a big, old, white washing machine

1 tall / dustbin / a / plastic / green
a tall, green, plastic dustbin

2 small / a / chair / Italian / round
a small, round, Italian chair

3 long / brown / shelf / a / wooden
a long, brown, wooden shelf

3 ★★★ **Complete Eleanor's article. Use her notes.**

My ideal classroom by Eleanor Bright
Computers – white, modern
Tables – plastic, low, round
Each desk has a Japanese TV – small and black
Leather armchairs – Italian and soft!
Cushions – cotton – large!
American fridge – very big

My ideal classroom has a lot of modern, white computers. There's one for every student. There aren't any desks but there are some low, (**1**) round, plastic tables. And each table has got a (**2**) small, black, Japanese TV too. Everybody sits in soft, (**3**) Italian, leather armchairs. If you want to relax, there are (**4**) large, cotton cushions. There's also a very (**5**) big, American fridge for snacks and drinks! And I almost forgot... . There's also a friendly, helpful teacher!

Writing Builder page 105

5 Characters

Vocabulary

Describing personality

1 ★ Complete the sentences. Use the words in the box.

ambitious   brave   cheerful   selfish   ~~talkative~~

He's very *talkative*.

1 She's not very cheerful.

2 She's quite selfish.

3 She's very brave.

4 He's very ambitious.

2 ★★ Choose the correct options.

He's quite *big-headed*. He thinks he's the best at everything.
a) brave   **b)** outgoing   **(c)** big-headed

1 She's very quiet. She never says much.
a) talkative   **(b)** quiet   **c)** hard-working

2 She's not at all shy. She loves meeting new people.
(a) shy   **b)** modest   **c)** selfish

3 He's not very cheerful. He never smiles.
a) miserable   **(b)** cheerful   **c)** ambitious

4 They're quite lazy. They don't help around the house at all.
a) bad-tempered   **b)** shy   **(c)** lazy

3 ★★ Complete the chart. Write the opposites of the words you chose in exercise 2. Use the words in the box.

hard-working   miserable   ~~modest~~   outgoing   talkative

Exercise 2	Opposites
big-headed	*modest*
(1) quiet	talkative
(2) shy	outgoing
(3) cheerful	miserable
(4) lazy	hard-working

4 ★★★ Complete true sentences about personalities.

My teacher's quite *cheerful*.

1 My brother's / sister's quite Students' answers.

2 My best friend isn't at all ___________ but she's very ___________.

3 My mum isn't very ___________ but she's quite ___________.

4 I'm very ___________ but I'm not at all ___________.

Comparative and superlative adjectives

1 ★ **Complete the chart. Use the words in the box.**

expensive funniest funny hotter hottest ~~longer~~ longest more expensive more selfish most selfish

Adjective	Comparative	Superlative
long	*longer*	the (1) longest
selfish	(2) more selfish	the (3) most selfish
(4) funny	funnier	the (5) funniest
(6) expensive	(7) more expensive	the most expensive
hot	(8) hotter	the (9) hottest

2 ★ **Choose the correct options.**

Summers in Spain are (**hotter**) / **hottest** than summers in England.

1 This shop's the **more** / (**most**) expensive in the whole city!

2 I think the **hotter** / (**hottest**) place on Earth is Al Aziziyah in Libya. On 13th September 1922 it was 57.8°C!

3 This is the **funnier** / (**funniest**) programme on TV at the moment.

4 Our new teacher's (**better**) / **best** than our last one.

5 Rob's the **more** / (**most**) selfish person I know.

6 My hair's (**longer**) / **longest** than my brother's.

7 This computer game's (**more**) / **most** expensive than all the others.

3 ★★ **Complete the sentences. Use the comparative forms of the adjectives in the box.**

bad ~~cold~~ exciting far important lazy quiet

The weather's *colder* than yesterday. I'm taking a jacket.

1 My brother's lazier than everyone in my family. He never helps with the housework.

2 I think happiness is more important than money.

3 The third *Harry Potter* film's more exciting than all the others. I loved it!

4 I live further from school than anyone else in my class.

5 My test marks this year are worse than last year!

6 I like living in the country. It's quieter than the city.

4 ★★ **Complete the sentences. Use superlatives and *in*.**

Teide, on Tenerife, is 3,718 metres high. It's *the highest mountain in* Spain.

1 The Fleurburger's an expensive burger. It costs $5,000. It's the most expensive burger in the world.

2 Windsor Castle's very big – 45,000 square metres. It's the biggest castle in the UK.

3 Vatican City is a very small country, with about 830 people. It's the smallest country in the world.

4 *Avatar* was a successful film because it earned more than $2 billion. It's the most successful film in history.

5 Andy Murray's a good tennis player but he isn't the best tennis player in the world.

6 Sultan Kosen from Turkey is 2.47 metres tall. He's the tallest man in the world.

 Grammar Bank pages 74–75

5 ★★★ **Compare Diego and Nina. Use the words in brackets.**

(healthy) Nina's healthier than Diego.

1 (thin) Diego's thinner than Nina.

2 (healthy) Nina's healthier than Diego.

3 (bad at English) Nina's worse at English than Diego.

4 (hard-working) Diego's more hard-working than Nina.

6 ★★★ **Write true sentences. Use the superlative forms of the adjectives in the box.**

fit good at computers heavy ~~musical~~ relaxed

My mum's the most musical person in my family.

1 Students' answers

2 ______

3 ______

4 ______

too and *enough*

7 ★ **Choose the correct options.**

You mustn't go to that area at night. It's **(too dangerous)** / **dangerous enough**.

1 I can't hear what he's saying. His voice isn't **too loud** / **(loud enough)**.

2 I'm not lending you my bike. You're not **too careful** / **(careful enough)**.

3 I didn't go swimming. It was **(too cold)** / **cold enough**.

8 ★★ **Complete the sentences. Use *too* or *enough* and the words in the box.**

brave busy ~~excited~~ fit jealous juicy

	Brett	Why didn't you sleep?
	Chris	I was too excited about the party.
1	**Paula**	Why didn't you go bungee jumping?
	Chris	I didn't feel brave enough !
2	**Brett**	Why did you break up with your boyfriend?
	Nicola	He was too jealous of my friends.
3	**Dad**	Why didn't you buy any oranges?
	Paula	They weren't juicy enough .
4	**Nicola**	Are you going to run in the marathon again?
	Paula	I can't. I'm not fit enough .
5	**Chris**	Can I ask you a question?
	Nicola	Sorry. I'm too busy at the moment.

9 ★★★ **Rewrite the underlined sentences. Use *too* or *enough* and the words in the box. Don't change the meanings.**

big-headed easy hard lazy ~~long~~ quiet warm

Can you write some more? Your essay's too short.
Your essay isn't long enough.

1 They don't get good marks. They aren't hard-working enough.
They're too lazy.

2 I don't want to live in England. It's too cold.
It isn't warm enough.

3 I'm going to do a different exercise. This one isn't hard enough.
This one's too easy.

4 I don't like him. He isn't modest enough.
He's too big-headed.

5 Can I buy another bed? This one's too soft.
This one isn't hard enough.

6 I can't work here. It's too noisy.
It isn't quiet enough.

Reading

1 Can you guess someone's personality from what they look like?

Face and personality

When we see someone's face for the first time, we often make an **instant** decision about their personality. For example, research shows that many people think beautiful people are more **outgoing**, intelligent and healthy. But can you really tell someone's personality from their face?

Some scientists think you can. It's called physiognomy. Ancient Greek philosophers wrote about it. And 150 years ago, people accepted it as scientific **fact**.

Now scientists are investigating physiognomy again. Canadian researchers studied the faces of men's ice hockey teams. They measured the widths of the players' faces and then compared this to how aggressive the players were. They found that wide-faced players were the most **aggressive**.

One magazine recently gave readers a questionnaire about their personalities. Readers also had to send in pictures of themselves. The magazine then put the faces on its website and people had to **guess** the personalities. Over 70 per cent of readers guessed the 'lucky' face and many guessed the 'honest' face.

And what about 'dishonest' faces? One robber says, 'I'm too ugly to get a job.' But don't worry. There are lots of ugly people with good jobs – and lots of criminals with great **looks**!

2 ★ Read the article. What is physiognomy about? Choose the best description.

(a) How personality is connected with facial features.
b) The typical personalities of good-looking people.
c) The personalities of people who play sport.

3 ★★ Match the words and the definitions.

	instant	**a)**	angry and ready to argue
1	outgoing	**b)**	how attractive someone is
2	fact	**c)**	friendly
3	aggressive	**d)**	something that is true
4	guess	**e)**	try to decide even if you don't know
5	looks	**f)**	immediate

4 ★★★ Answer the questions.

What do many people think about beautiful people's personalities?
They think they're more outgoing, intelligent and healthy.

1 What is physiognomy?
How to tell someone's personality from their face.

2 What did people think about physiognomy 150 years ago?
They believed it was true.

3 What did researchers in Canada compare?
They compared the widths of ice-hockey players' faces and how aggressive the players were.

4 What kinds of personalities do people guess easily from faces?
People guess lucky personalities and honest personalities easily.

5 Are criminals always ugly?
No. There are lots of criminals with great looks.

Compound adjectives

1 ★ **Match the words and the pictures.**

big-nosed broad-shouldered dark-haired
high-heeled ~~long-sleeved~~ thin-lipped

a long-sleeved shirt

1 a broad-shouldered boy

2 a dark-haired girl

3 high-heeled shoes

4 a thin-lipped man

5 a big-nosed woman

2 ★★ **Rewrite the sentences. Use compound adjectives. Don't change the meanings.**

She's a girl with quick wits.
She's a quick-witted girl.

1 My sister's the girl with green eyes.
My sister's the green-eyed girl.

2 I bought a shirt with short sleeves.
I bought a short-sleeved shirt.

3 The chair with the high back is very comfortable.
The high-backed chair is very comfortable.

4 Tom's the boy with broad shoulders.
Tom's the broad-shouldered boy.

5 Bart Simpson's a boy with yellow skin.
Bart Simpson's a yellow-skinned boy.

6 I don't like David because he's a boy with a loud mouth.
I don't like David because he's a loud-mouthed boy.

3 ★★★ **Complete true sentences. Use compound adjectives.**

My best friend's a kind-hearted person.

1 I'm Students' answers ______.

2 My mum's ______.

3 My dad's ______.

4 My teacher's ______.

5 My brother's / sister's ______.

6 My aunt / uncle is ______.

Describing people

1 ★ **Put the sentences in the correct order.**

Amy That's Jim's sister. Her name's Cassy. 5
Amy I'm not in the photo. I took it! 9
Amy That's Jim. It was his barbecue. 3
Amy Look at this photo. It's from my friend's barbecue. 1
Amy Really? She isn't! She's really relaxed. 7
Jess What about the long-haired girl in the short-sleeved dress? 4
Jess She looks really bad-tempered. 6
Jess Who's the broad-shouldered boy in the middle? 2
Jess So where are you? 8

2 ★★ **Answer the questions.**

What is the photo of?
It's of Amy's friend's barbecue.

1 Who's the boy with broad shoulders?
Jim.

2 What does Cassy look like?
She's got long hair and she looks really bad-tempered.

3 What's Cassy's personality like?
She's really relaxed.

4 Where's Amy in the photo?
She isn't in the photo.

3 ★★★ **Write a dialogue in your notebook like the dialogue in exercise 1. Use the picture.**

Dictation

4 ★★ 4.06 **Listen. Listen again and write the sentences in your notebook.**

Describing a fictional character

1 ★ **Are the sentences correct or incorrect? Write ✓ or ✗.**

I had a bath and felt better. ✓

1 She's ambitious but also quite modest. ✓
2 We cleaned the floor because was dirty. ✗
3 He often makes mistakes even though is very clever. ✗
4 They live here but go to school in the city. ✓
5 It's a long-legged spider and lives in Asia. ✓

2 ★★ **Cross out the extra pronouns. Tick (✓) the sentences with no extra pronouns.**

Sylar's tall and ~~he~~ has dark brown eyes.
He's very dangerous because he has special powers. ✓

1 Maggie Simpson can't talk but ~~she~~ can walk.
2 She's yellow-skinned and ~~she's~~ always sucking a dummy.
3 Betty Suarez wears unfashionable clothes even though she works at a fashion magazine. ✓
4 Betty Suarez is kind-hearted unless she gets annoyed. ✓

3 ★★★ **Complete the description of Meredith Grey. Use the notes.**

TV series: *Grey's Anatomy*, about a group of hospital doctors, very popular
Name: Meredith Grey (main character)

1 Appearance: fair skin; long, brown hair; blue eyes
2 Personality: ambitious; also kind-hearted
3 Why I like her character: I want to be a great doctor, like her!

Grey's Anatomy is a TV series about a group of hospital doctors and is very popular. Meredith Grey is the main character. (**1**) She's fair-skinned and has got long, brown hair and blue eyes. (**2**) She's ambitious but also kind-hearted and hard-working. (**3**) I like her character because I want to be a great doctor, like her!

Writing Builder page 106

6 Danger!

Vocabulary

Adventure sports

1 ★ **Match the photos and the words in the box.**

bungee jumping kayaking kite surfing rock climbing skydiving ~~snorkelling~~ waterskiing windsurfing

snorkelling

4 bungee jumping

1 skydiving

5 waterskiing

2 windsurfing

6 rock climbing

3 kayaking

7 kite surfing

2 ★★ **Complete the words. Match the words and the pictures.**

s k y d i v i n g a)

1 k a y a k i n g f)

2 w a t e r s k i i n g c)

3 b u n g e e j u m p i n g b)

4 s n o r k e l l i n g e)

5 w i n d s u r f i n g d)

a)

d)

b)

e)

c)

f)

3 ★★★ **Answer the questions.**

For which sport do you need:

the wind? windsurfing

1 a hard hat and a light? caving

2 walls and buildings? free running

3 wings and the sky? hang-gliding

4 very high buildings or mountains? BASE jumping

5 mountains and ropes? rock climbing

Vocabulary Bank pages 94–95

Present perfect affirmative and negative

1 ★ **Complete the chart. Use the words in the box.**

~~been~~ did do drank drunk finish finished hear heard ran ridden rode run tried try written wrote

Base form	Past simple	Past participle
be	was / were	*been*
(1) *do*	(2) *did*	done
drink	(3) *drank*	(4) *drunk*
(5) *finish*	finished	(6) *finished*
(7) *hear*	(8) *heard*	heard
ride	(9) *rode*	(10) *ridden*
(11) *run*	(12) *ran*	run
(13) *try*	tried	(14) *tried*
write	(15) *wrote*	(16) *written*

2 ★ **Choose the correct options.**

Jenny and I haven't ever **(ridden)** / **rode** a motorbike.

1 Ruth and I **has** / **(have)** tried windsurfing.
2 Simon has **(drunk)** / **drank** all the orange juice.
3 Martha and Tim have **ran** / **(run)** over ten kilometres this week.
4 I **('ve)** / **'s** sent six emails today.
5 Tom **(hasn't)** / **haven't** heard this song before.
6 Sally and Joe still **(haven't)** / **hasn't** finished their project.
7 It's **was** / **(been)** sunny all day.
8 Dad hasn't **did** / **(done)** any work today.

3 ★★ **Complete the sentences. Use the present perfect of the verbs in the box.**

find / lose make / do meet / speak ~~read~~ / see write / send

1 I*'ve read* three *Harry Potter* books and I *'ve seen* all the films.
2 We *'ve made* dinner and we *'ve done* the housework.
3 The children *have written* their 'thank you' letters and they *'ve sent* them.
4 Jim *'s found* his keys. They were under his bed. Now he *'s lost* his glasses!
5 I *'ve met* two famous people and I *'ve spoken* to them.

4 ★★ **Complete the text. Use the present perfect of the verbs in brackets.**

You*'ve* probably *seen* (see) Sébastian Foucan in films or TV adverts but you probably *haven't heard* (**1** not hear) of him. Sébastian is a free runner and he *'s become* (**2** become) one of the world's best free runners. In 2003, Sébastian made a film with two other free runners. They *'ve* also *made* (**3** make) two documentaries about free running and they *'ve jumped* (**4** jump) over several places, from Edinburgh Castle to football stadiums. Sébastian *has* also *appeared* (**5** appear) in many films, such as *Casino Royale*, and he and other free runners *have danced* (**6** dance) with Madonna in her concerts.

But is free running dangerous? 'Of course,' says another free runner. 'But I *'ve done* (**7** do) it for years. And so far, I *haven't broken* (**8** not break) any bones!'

Grammar Bank pages 76–77

5 ★★★ **Write true sentences about you and the people you know. Use the present perfect affirmative or negative and the ideas in the box.**

> climb a tree do somebody a favour today
> have an argument today
> have a meal out this month
> ~~read an English magazine~~
> send a text to a teacher win a competition

I haven't read an English magazine.

1 Students' answers
2 ______
3 ______
4 ______
5 ______
6 ______

Present perfect with *just*

6 ★ **Complete the sentences. Use the words in the boxes.**

> 's just started 's just left ~~'ve just been~~

	Tom	*I've just been* on an adventure sports holiday.
	Rob	Really? What did you do?
1	**Ann**	Steve 's just left.
	Leigh	Oh no! I wanted to see him.
2	**Pam**	It 's just started raining.
	Alan	Oh no! The washing's outside.

> have just gone 've just had 've just tried

3	**Tom**	We 've just tried kayaking.
	Rob	Wow! Was it exciting?
4	**Ann**	You 've just had lunch!
	Leigh	I know. But I'm still hungry.
5	**Pam**	Macy and Pete have just gone home.
	Alan	Why? It's still early.

7 ★★ **Complete the sentences. Use *just* and the present perfect affirmative of the verbs in the box.**

> do climb ~~finish~~ have make

He's *just finished* his homework.

1 They 've just climbed a mountain.

2 She 's just done the shopping.

3 They 've just had an argument.

4 He 's just made a mistake.

8 ★★★ **Answer the questions. Use your own ideas. Use the present perfect affirmative and *just*.**

	Tina	Are you hungry?
	Bev	No, *I've just had dinner.*
1	**Jo**	Are your parents at home?
	Paul	No, Students' answers.
2	**Bev**	Where's Sarah?
	Paul	She ______.
3	**Jo**	Why do you look so pleased?
	Tina	I ______.

1 **How long can you hold your breath?**

Take a deep breath …

Most people can hold their breath for about 40 seconds. Tanya Streeter can do it for over six minutes!

In 1997, Tanya lived in the Caribbean. On Saturdays she went fishing with spears. She could swim underwater for a long time. So, one day she went to a free-diving class. Free-diving is diving without breathing equipment. Fishermen have done free-diving for years, looking for pearls. Now, it's an international sport.

Tanya dived to 30 metres in her first lesson. She was a natural free-diver. Her teacher persuaded her to train with him and just a few months later she was breaking world records.

In 2002, Tanya broke the record for the deepest dive by anyone – 160 metres! At this depth, the water pressure's very high. Your lungs are the size of a baby's hand and the pain in your ears is sharp. There's no light. Divers can easily become unconscious. However, Tanya believes that it's safe if you train carefully and have the correct equipment.

The men's free-diving record is now 214 metres! Tanya still has the world record for women's free-diving. She has also presented TV programmes on diving with sharks, showing environmental problems in our seas.

2 ★ **Read the text. Why is Tanya Streeter famous?**

She broke the record for the deepest dive. / She has the world record for women's free-diving.

3 ★★ **Are these sentences true or false? Write T or F.**

Tanya can stay underwater for almost six minutes. F

1 Fishermen started free-diving in 1997. F
2 Tanya's teacher thought she was very good at free-diving. T
3 At 160 metres under the sea, it's difficult to see. T
4 Tanya still has the record for the deepest free-dive made by anyone. F
5 Tanya's interested in the environment. T

4 ★★★ **Answer the questions.**

Why did Tanya go to a free-diving class?
She could swim underwater for a long time.

1 Why do some fishermen free-dive?
Because they are looking for pearls.

2 How deep did Tanya dive in her first lesson?
She dived to 30 metres.

3 What are two problems for divers in deep water?
The water pressure is very high. Your lungs are very small. Your ears hurt. There isn't any light. Divers can easily become unconscious. (Any two)

4 What world record does Tanya still hold?
She holds the world record for women's free-diving.

5 What other thing has Tanya done?
She has presented TV programmes.

Adjective opposites

1 ★ **Write the opposites. Use the words in the box.**

clean dark dry heavy quiet sharp
smooth ~~soft~~ soft strong wide

hard *soft*

1 loud quiet
2 weak strong
3 narrow wide
4 blunt sharp
5 dirty clean
6 wet dry
7 light dark and heavy
8 rough smooth and soft

2 ★★ **Complete the sentences. Use one from each pair in the box.**

blunt / ~~sharp~~ dirty / clean dry / wet
high / low light / dark light / heavy
shallow / deep strong / weak wide / narrow

Be careful with that knife. It's very *sharp*.

1 Can you help me with these bags? I'm not strong enough.
2 You can't dive here. The water's too shallow.
3 We can't drive down this street. It's too narrow.
4 That isn't Dan. His hair's dark, not fair.
5 **Jack** Why are you so wet?
Tim It's raining outside!
6 There are a lot of dirty dishes in the sink. Can you wash up?
7 **Sam** Why are you walking so strangely?
Tracy It's these shoes. The heels are too high.
8 Can you help me carry this table? It's very heavy.

3 ★★ **Write adjectives to describe the pictures.**

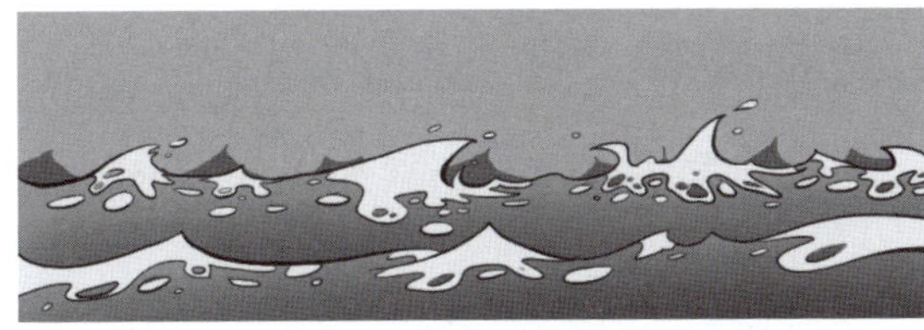

deep, wet

1 Possible answers: blunt, heavy, sharp

2 Possible answers: soft, smooth, small

3 Possible answers: wet, dirty

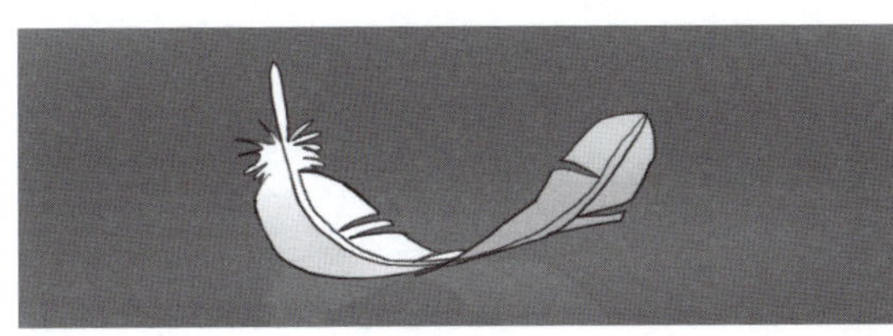

4 Possible answers: light, soft

4 ★★★ **Write two things that can be:**

blunt or sharp
knives, pencils

1 narrow and dark
Students' answers
2 rough or smooth
3 dry and rough
4 high or low

Talking about experiences

1 ★ **Complete the dialogue. Use the words in the box.**

> amazing ~~been~~ like never that to try tried went

Dylan	Have you ever *been* snorkelling?
Grace	No, I haven't. Have you?
Dylan	Yes. I **(1)** went snorkelling last summer.
Grace	Where was **(2)** that ?
Dylan	In the Medes Islands in Spain.
Grace	What was it **(3)** like ?
Dylan	It was really **(4)** amazing . Have you **(5)** tried any other water sports?
Grace	No, I've **(6)** never done any water sports, but I've been caving.
Dylan	Really? I'd love **(7)** to try caving. It looks really exciting!

2 ★★ **Answer the questions.**

Has Dylan ever been snorkelling?
Yes, he has.

1 Has Grace ever been snorkelling?
No, she hasn't.

2 When did Dylan go snorkelling?
Last summer.

3 Where did he do it?
In the Medes Islands in Spain.

4 What adventure sport has Grace tried?
She's tried caving.

5 What does Dylan think about caving?
He thinks it looks really exciting.

3 ★★★ **Write a dialogue in your notebook like the dialogue in exercise 1. Use the ideas in the box.**

> Lily – kayaking – two years ago – Canada – fantastic
> Oliver – bungee jumping – scary

Dictation

4 ★★ 4.07 **Listen. Listen again and write the sentences in your notebook.**

Postcard

1 ★ **Complete the chart. Use the words in the box.**

> ~~be broke~~ friends frightening guy ~~have no money~~ loads of lots of man / boy mates scary

Formal	Informal
have no money	*be broke*
friends	mates
frightening	scary
man / boy	guy
lots of	loads of

2 ★★ **Complete the messages. Use the informal equivalents of the words in the box.**

> ~~fabulous~~ friend frightening haven't got any money lots of man quite television

Kat	I've just watched a *fab* programme on **(1)** telly . It was about a **(2)** guy who was a vampire. It was really **(3)** scary .
Amy	It sounds **(4)** pretty cool. Are you coming out tomorrow night?
Kat	I can't. I **(5)** 'm broke .
Amy	I've got **(6)** loads of money at the moment. I'll lend you some.
Kat	Really? Thanks! You're a **(7)** mate !

3 ★★★ **Complete the informal postcard.**

Hi Mum, hi Dad,
I've had a **fab** week on holiday and I've made (1) loads of really good (2) mates . I've learned to windsurf and I haven't watched (3) telly once! Yesterday we went kite surfing. I loved it but it was a bit (4) scary . The (5) guys who teach us are really cool.

Love, Tom

PS It's (6) pretty expensive here and I (7) 'm broke . Can you send me some money?

Writing Builder page 107

7 Out and about

Vocabulary

In the high street

1 ★ Complete the words.

baker's

1 b o o k s h o p
2 ch e m i s t's
3 cl o t h e s sh o p
4 el e c t r i c a l st o r e
5 h a i r d r e ss e r's
6 p o s t o ff i c e

2 ★★ Complete the crossword.

The place where you …

1 … arrange a holiday.
2 → … take out, borrow or deposit money.
2 ↓ … buy meat.
3 … buy flowers.
4 … buy cooked food to eat at home.
5 … can see houses for sale.
6 … buy magazines.

3 ★★ Which of the places in exercise 2 do you write with an apostrophe (')?

travel agent's

1 butcher's
2 florist's
3 estate agent's
4 newsagent's

4 ★★★ Read the shop names. Write the type of shop for each name.

florist's

1 bookshop

2 baker's

3 takeaway

4 electrical store

5 hairdresser's

6 clothes shop

Present perfect interrogative

1 ★ **Choose the correct options.**

	Chris	**Has** / **(Have)** I met your brother?
	Greg	Yes, **you've** / **(you have!)**
1	**Sue**	Have you and Tim **did** / **(done)** the housework?
	Julie	Yes, we **(have)** / **haven't.**
2	**Rob**	**(Has)** / **Have** Sara phoned you today?
	Dawn	Yes, she **(has)** / **haven't.**
3	**Sue**	Has the film **finish** / **(finished?)**
	Chris	Yes, it **(has)** / **have.**
4	**Rob**	Have you **drove** / **(driven)** a car?
	Dawn	No, I **hasn't** / **(haven't.)**
5	**Greg**	Has your brother **sells** / **(sold)** his computer?
	Julie	No, he **has** / **(hasn't.)**
6	**Rob**	**Has** / **(Have)** you used all the milk?
	Greg	Yes, **we've** / **(we have.)**
7	**Sue**	**Has** / **(Have)** you and Jess spent all your money?
	Dawn	No, we **have** / **(haven't.)**

2 ★★ **Complete the sentences. Use the present perfect.**

Have you seen (you / see) my sister?
Yes, I *have*.

1 Have I made (I / make) a mistake?
Yes, you have.

2 Has it stopped (it / stop) raining?
No, it hasn't.

3 Have your parents bought (your parents / buy) a new car?
Yes, they have.

4 Have you eaten (you / eat) my sandwich?
No, we haven't.

5 Has Simon read (Simon / read) this book?
No, he hasn't.

3 ★★ **Correct the mistakes.**

Has your sister gone to bed? Yes, ~~she's~~.
she has

1 Have you ~~spoke~~ to your grandmother recently? No, I haven't. spoken

2 Has Dad ~~fix~~ my computer? Yes, he has. fixed

3 Have you finished your dinner? No, we ~~aren't~~. haven't

4 ~~Has~~ Simon and Ellie done their homework? No, they haven't. Have

5 Have you ~~took~~ my pen? Yes, I have. taken

4 ★★★ **Write questions and short answers. Use the information in the chart.**

	Ben	Mary and Paul
do any work	✓	(1) ✗
have a shower	(2) ✗	✗
check email	✓	(3) ✗
send any texts	(4) ✓	✗
see any friends	✗	(5) ✓

Has Ben done any work today?
Yes, he has.

1 Have Mary and Paul done any work today?
No, they haven't.

2 Has Ben had a shower today?
No, he hasn't.

3 Have Mary and Paul checked their email today?
No, they haven't.

4 Has Ben sent any texts today?
Yes, he has.

5 Have Mary and Paul seen any friends today?
Yes, they have.

Grammar Bank pages 78–79

How long ...?; *for* and *since*

5 ★ **Put the words in the correct order.**

have / you / a computer? / had / How long
How long have you had a computer?
Since 2007.

1 has / at university? / How long / been / your sister
How long has your sister been at university?

Since October.

2 Mr Thomas / How long / been / has / your teacher?
How long has Mr Thomas been your teacher?

For six months.

3 have / played the guitar? / How long / you
How long have you played the guitar?

Since I was seven.

4 your mum / has / done yoga? / How long
How long has your mum done yoga?

For three years.

6 ★ **Complete the chart. Use the phrases in the box.**

~~a long time~~ a year I got up nine o'clock ten minutes three weeks Thursday 2002

For	Since
a long time	(4) I got up
(1) a year	(5) nine o'clock
(2) ten minutes	(6) Thursday
(3) three weeks	(7) 2002

7 ★★ **Write questions with *How long ...?* Write true answers with *for* or *since*.**

How long / you and your parents / live / in your house or flat? (for)
How long have you and your parents lived in your house or flat?
We've lived in our flat for six years.

1 How long / you / be / at your school? (since)
How long have you been at your school?
Students' answers

2 How long / you / have / your English teacher? (for)
How long have you had your English teacher?

3 How long / your best friend / know / you? (for)
How long has your best friend known you?

4 How long / you and your friends / use / *Switch*? (since)
How long have you and your friends used *Switch*?

8 ★★★ **Write questions with *How long ...?* Write answers with *for* or *since*.**

I started at this school three years ago. (be at this school, for)
How long have you been at this school?
I've been at this school for three years.

1 Stacy moved to London in 2003. (live in London, since)
How long has Stacy lived in London?
She's lived in London since 2003.

2 We got our computer at Christmas. (had a computer, since)
How long have you had a computer?
We've had a computer since Christmas.

3 Mr Taylor became a Spanish teacher twelve years ago. (teach Spanish, for)
How long has Mr Taylor taught Spanish?
He's taught Spanish for twelve years.

Reading

1 **What are your parents' rules about you going out alone?**

Help! Let me out!

How strict are your parents? Can you go out alone? Do your parents always know where you are?

A recent survey in England is worrying some experts. It reveals that 30 per cent of children between twelve and sixteen hardly ever go out alone. Their parents are too frightened that it's dangerous.

'Playing outside, with other children, is an extremely important part of children's development,' says Robert Carr from the Children's Society. 'At the moment, children spend too much time alone, playing computer games or watching telly.'

The problem, Robert believes, is that children aren't developing their social skills. They're becoming shyer and less outgoing.

Medical experts are also worried. When children stay at home in their free time, they often don't exercise as much. This means health problems. What do you think? Are parents being overprotective or just sensible in a modern world?

Comments

I prefer staying at home to going out. But I'm not shy! *Deb*

Our world's a dangerous place. Of course I let my children out. But I'm always with them. *Henry*

This is so true. Parents should talk to children about safety and going out, but children aren't prisoners. They need more freedom! *Mark*

2 ★ **Read the article. What's its main topic?**

a) Why some children are becoming overweight.

b) Hobbies you can do at home.

c) A survey about children and going out alone.

3 ★★ **Are these sentences true or false? Write T or F.**

Almost a third of children between twelve and sixteen never go out. F

1 Robert Carr thinks children should play more computer games. F

2 Robert thinks children are becoming less sociable. T

3 Medical experts are worried because some children aren't doing enough exercise. T

4 Deb agrees with the article. F

5 Henry's children never go out alone. T

6 Mark agrees with the article. T

4 ★★★ **Answer the questions.**

Why are some experts worried about the survey?

Because 30 per cent of children between twelve and sixteen hardly ever go out alone.

1 Why don't some parents allow their children to go out?

They are too frightened that it's dangerous.

2 What does Robert Carr think is happening to the personalities of children who stay in too much?

They are becoming shyer and less outgoing.

3 What other problems can it cause? Why?

It can cause health problems because children don't exercise as much.

4 Does Henry permit his children to go out?

Yes, he does, but he's always with them.

5 What does Mark think that parents should do?

He thinks parents should talk to children about safety and going out.

Synonyms and antonyms

1 ★ **Are the words synonyms or antonyms? Write S or A.**

attractive / ugly A
1 start / begin S
2 loud / noisy S
3 dry / wet A

2 ★★ **Replace the underlined words. Use the words in the boxes.**

Synonyms
correct extremely hard ~~store~~

We went to the shop to buy eggs. *store*
1 I was incredibly tired last night. extremely
2 You've made a mistake. That's not right. correct
3 I can't do this exercise. It's really difficult. hard

Antonyms
fast quiet sharp

4 My computer's really slow. fast
5 This knife's very blunt. sharp
6 The music's too loud. quiet

3 ★★★ **Replace one word in each sentence so that it makes sense. Use antonyms.**

The homework was very ~~difficult~~. I finished it in ten minutes! *easy*
1 Careful! That knife's very ~~blunt~~. sharp
2 He's very ~~slow~~. He can run 100 metres in under twelve seconds. fast
3 You're extremely ~~dry~~! Is it raining outside? wet

4 ★★★ **Replace one word in each sentence. Use synonyms.**

I'm ~~extremely~~ interested in your idea. incredibly
1 The delivery's very ~~quick~~ at that takeaway. fast
2 I'm going to the ~~store~~ if you want anything. shop
3 It was a great film but we were very ~~scared~~. frightened

False friends

5 ★ **Choose the correct options.**

Your complexion describes:
a) your body (b) your face
1 A vase is for:
(a) flowers b) drinks
2 A sane person is:
a) physically healthy (b) mentally healthy
3 A recluse is someone who:
a) is in prison
(b) doesn't like being with other people
4 Actually means:
a) currently (b) really
5 An exit is:
(a) the door for leaving a place
b) a success

6 ★★ **Complete the words.**

There's ink on the *carpet*. Mum will be angry!
1 I love the f abric of your dress. Is it cotton?
2 Hello, Tom. It's your Uncle Mark. Are your p arents at home?
3 Please leave the building through the door that says 'E xit'.
4 Sally can go to the shop alone. She's very s ensible.
5 Your workbook's completely b lank. Why haven't you done any of the exercises?

7 ★★★ **Choose the correct replies.**

Gina What happened to your carpet?
Clare (a) I dropped a drink on it.
b) I left it at school.

1 **Tim** Have you got any blank paper?
Kerry a) No, I've only got blue paper.
(b) No, I've only got paper with lines.

2 **Gina** Is your young brother quite sensible?
Sean (a) Yes, he never does anything silly.
b) Yes, he cries very easily.

3 **Glen** Sally's pretending to be a doctor.
Clare a) Is she going to medical school?
(b) My sister loves playing games too.

Making plans

1 ★ **Put the sentences in the correct order.**

Lisa	Then afterwards, we're going to go swimming. 7
Lisa	Well, Danny and I are going to go shopping. Do you want to come along? 3
Lisa	Ten o'clock at Danny's house. 9
Lisa	What are your plans for Saturday morning? 1
Lisa	We're going to the new shopping centre near Danny's house. 5
Chris	OK. See you on Saturday morning. 10
Chris	I haven't got any, really. Why? 2
Chris	That sounds great. 6
Chris	Yes, I'd love to. Where are you going to go? 4
Chris	Great. What time shall we meet? 8

2 ★★ **Answer the questions.**

What are Chris's plans for Saturday morning?
He hasn't got any plans.

1 Where is the shopping centre?
Near Danny's house.

2 What are Lisa and Danny going to do after going shopping?
They're going to go swimming.

3 What time are the friends meeting?
At ten o'clock.

4 Where are the friends meeting?
At Danny's house.

3 ★★★ **Write a dialogue in your notebook like the dialogue in exercise 1. Use Damon's notes.**

Sunday morning: rollerblading with Susie in the park (meet at Susie's house 9 a.m.). Lunch at my house. Invite Rick!

Dictation

4 ★★ 4.08 **Listen. Listen again and write the sentences in your notebook.**

Informal letter

1 ★ **Choose the correct options.**

1 Jess has got my school bag. I left **its** / **it** at **her** / **she** house.

2 I've known George since we were babies. **Us** / **Our** parents were neighbours. **We** / **Us** were born on the same day.

3 That's our new teacher, Mr Turner. Do you know **he** / **him**? **He** / **His** can be very strict!

4 Have you been to that new clothes shop? **It** / **Its** name is 'Guys' and **it** / **its** sells clothes for teenage boys.

2 ★★ **Rewrite the underlined words. Avoid repeating nouns.**

Amy has got two sisters. Her sisters' names are Emma and Daisy. Their

1 Alfie and I love old music. Alfie and my favourite group's the Beatles. Our

2 Do you like my trousers? I bought my trousers at the market. them

3 Jen is Rob's sister. Rob's older than Jen. He's, her

4 Evie and Millie don't like football. Evie and Millie think football's boring. They, it's

3 ★★★ **Complete the informal letter.**

Dear Uncle James and Aunt Mel,

At the weekend we're going on holiday to Spain. Mary's really excited. She hasn't ever been on a plane. We're going to stay in a place in the mountains. (1) Its *name's Busquitar. I've read some guide books about the area. (2)* They *say it's really interesting.*

Do you remember my friend, John? (3) He *'s going to come with us. (4)* His *parents aren't coming. (5)* They *'re going to stay here in England. It's his first holiday without his parents. I think (6)* he *'s probably a bit nervous!*

Love,

Michael xx

Writing Builder page 108

8 Into the future

Vocabulary

High-tech gadgets

1 ★ **Circle the words. Use the words to say what people need in the pictures.**

P	H	O	T	O	F	R	A	M	E	M
F	P	K	W	I	R	E	L	E	S	S
E	G	L	S	D	W	A	W	I	F	J
F	M	K	A	B	B	E	N	Z	L	K
G	H	Y	T	Y	N	S	W	L	G	A
A	T	U	Z	B	E	S	S	I	D	N
L	K	F	B	L	U	R	A	Y	Y	W

USB hub

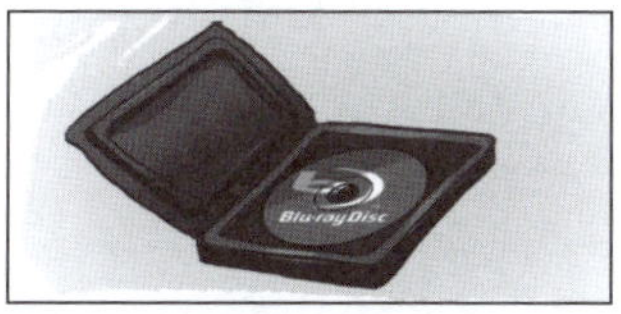

1 Blu-ray player

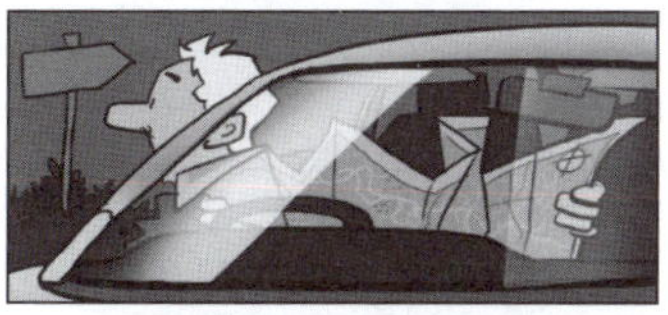

2 sat nav

3 wireless headset

4 MP3 player

5 digital photo frame

2 ★★ **Complete the crossword.**

Something you need to …

1 … find directions.
2 … record TV programmes.
3 … watch TV.
4 … play video games.
5 … make a film.
6 … connect lots of computer devices.
7 … connect a TV to a DVD recorder.
8 … listen to lots of radio stations.

	1 S		2 D								3 L	
	A		V								C	
	T		D								D	
	N		R								T	
4 G	A	M	E	S	5 C	O	N	S	O	L	E	
	V		C		A						L	
6 U			O		M						E	
7 S	C	A	R	T	C	A	B	L	E		V	
B			D		O						I	
H			E		R						S	
U			R		8 D	A	B	R	A	D	I	O
B					E						O	
					R						N	

3 ★★★ **Write definitions.**

A DVD player
Something you use to play DVDs.

1 a Blu-ray player
Something you use to play Blu-ray discs.

2 a wireless headset
Something you use to talk on your mobile phone while driving.

3 a plasma TV
Something you use to watch television.

4 an MP3 player
Something you use to play music.

will

1 ★ **Are these predictions affirmative, negative or interrogative? Write A, N or I.**

In 50 years …
… everyone will have an email address. A

1 … will there be any wires in our houses? I
2 … Spain won't win the World Cup. N
3 … I think it'll rain a lot more. A
4 … will students use books at school? I
5 … there won't be any diseases. N

2 ★★ **Complete the sentences. Use *will* or *won't* and the verbs in the box.**

be	buy	~~start~~	wear	tidy

I think she'll start walking soon.

1 He won't wear the trousers.

2 I think he 'll tidy his room soon.

3 It won't be sunny tomorrow.

4 I think they 'll buy a sat nav soon.

3 ★★ **Write questions for the answers.**

Will you be famous one day?
Yes, I'll be famous one day.

1 Will Sally do well in the test?
No, Sally won't do well in the test.

2 Will you do the ironing on Saturday?
Yes, we'll do the ironing on Saturday.

3 Will you go to the post office?
No, we won't go to the post office.

4 Will Tom bring his games console?
Yes, Tom will bring his games console.

5 Will it rain tomorrow?
No, it won't rain tomorrow.

6 Will you be at home tonight?
No, I won't be at home tonight.

7 Will your parents take me home?
Yes, my parents will take you home.

4 ★★★ **Make predictions about you and people you know in five years' time. Use the verbs in the box.**

~~be~~	have	live	own	play	study	work

I'll be at university.

1 Students' answers
2 ______
3 ______
4 ______
5 ______
6 ______

Grammar Bank pages 80–81

First conditional

5 ★ **Choose the correct options.**

If you don't come to my party, I **don't** / **won't** invite you again.

1 If you **write** / **'ll write** it in your diary, you won't forget it.

2 If I don't understand the homework, **I** / **I'll** phone you.

3 If **we** / **we'll** play music too loudly, we'll wake up the baby.

4 If they're vegetarians, I **won't** / **don't** cook meat.

5 If **I'll** / **I** see your brother, I'll tell him to call you.

6 If you **eat** / **'ll eat** a lot of chocolate, you'll get a bad complexion.

6 ★★ **Complete the sentences. Use the first conditional of the pairs of verbs in the box.**

become / not speak go / buy ~~have / have to~~
move / not see not help / not give
not leave / be walk / see
want / need

If we *have* a meal out, you'll *have to* pay.

1 If I move to Madrid, I won't see you any more.

2 If you walk towards the cinema, you 'll see the bookshop on your right.

3 If he becomes famous, he won't speak to us any more.

4 If he doesn't help at home, I won't give him any pocket money.

5 If they don't leave soon, they 'll be late.

6 If I go to the post office, I 'll buy you some stamps.

7 If you want to use your mobile phone in the car, you 'll need a wireless headset.

7 ★★ **Write first conditional sentences.**

Sara / make / dinner / I / wash up

If Sara makes dinner, I'll wash up.

1 Rick / not work / hard enough / he / not pass / his exam

If Rick doesn't work hard enough, he won't pass his exam.

2 my jeans / not be / dirty / I / wear / them to the party

If my jeans aren't dirty, I'll wear them to the party.

3 you / buy / a Blu-ray player / you / need / a new TV

If you buy a Blu-ray player, you'll need a new TV.

4 my parents / buy / a sat nav / they / not get / lost again

If my parents buy a sat nav, they won't get lost again.

5 we / go / on holiday / I / send / you a postcard

If we go on holiday, I'll send you a postcard.

8 ★★★ **Complete the first conditional sentences with your own ideas. Use the affirmative (A) or negative (N).**

If I don't go out this weekend, *I'll finish my book.* (A)

1 If my friend doesn't call me tonight, Students' answers ______. (N)

2 If school doesn't open tomorrow, ______. (A)

3 If you don't tell me the secret, ______. (N)

4 If my brother doesn't come home tonight, ______. (A)

5 If I try to learn another language, ______. (A)

6 If I don't get a birthday present from my parents, ______. (N)

Reading

1 Have you heard of any Spanish inventors? What did they invent?

Inventions that could change the world!

1 Many people have wireless Internet connections and wireless headsets. But all electrical equipment needs power and, therefore, power cables or batteries. However, scientists are working to change this. They've already shown wireless electricity with a light bulb, lighting it without any wires or batteries. This is WiTricity – the name for wireless electricity.

2 Electric vehicles are often slow and can't travel very far. What about a car that costs almost nothing to run? A Japanese company say they've invented a water-powered car. But they won't say how it works. They say that if you put a litre of water in it, it'll drive for one hour. Many scientists don't believe them. 'This isn't going to happen in the next five or even ten years,' says Jim Holding, from the UK Energy Centre.

3 What's the most important liquid on Earth? No, it isn't oil. It's drinking water. Water covers 70 per cent of the Earth but one billion people don't have enough drinking water. Six thousand people die every day from drinking dirty water. However, a Swiss company says the LifeStraw will change that. Their invention removes dangerous bacteria from dirty water. Each straw costs five euros and lasts for three years.

a)

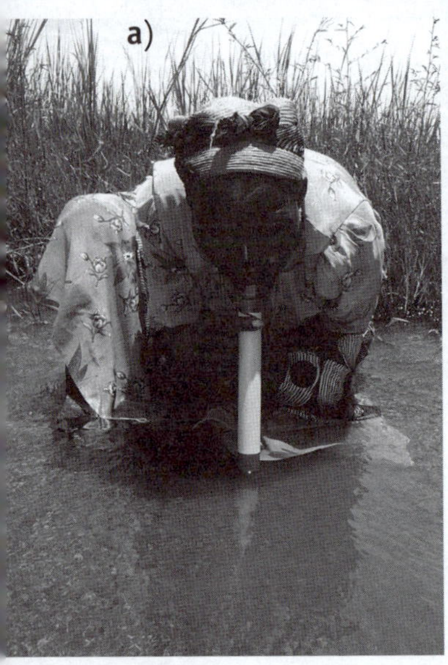

b)

c)

2 (★) **Read the text. Match the pictures and the paragraphs.**

1 b) 2 c) 3 a)

3 (★★) **Are these sentences true or false? Write T or F.**

Wireless headsets use WiTricity. F

1. Scientists have given up developing wireless electricity. F
2. Electric vehicles don't travel very fast. T
3. The inventors of water-powered cars are keeping the technology secret. T
4. Jim Holding believes a water-powered car is possible in five years. F
5. The most important liquid on Earth is drinking water. T
6. Almost a billion people die from drinking dirty water every year. F
7. The LifeStraw can be used five times. F

4 (★★★) **Answer the questions.**

What is WiTricity?
It's a way of giving power to devices without using wires.

1. What have scientists already done with WiTricity?
   They have lit a light bulb without wires or batteries.
2. What are the disadvantages of electric vehicles?
   They are often slow and can't travel very far.
3. How many litres of water does the water-powered car need to travel for one hour?
   It needs one litre of water.
4. How many people die every day because they don't have enough drinking water?
   Six thousand people die every day.
5. What does the LifeStraw do?
   It removes dangerous bacteria from dirty water.
6. How long can you use a LifeStraw for?
   You can use a LifeStraw for three years.

Phrasal verbs

1 ★ **Match the phrases and the pictures.**

give in　give out　put on
take off　~~turn off~~　turn on

turn off

1 turn on

2 take off

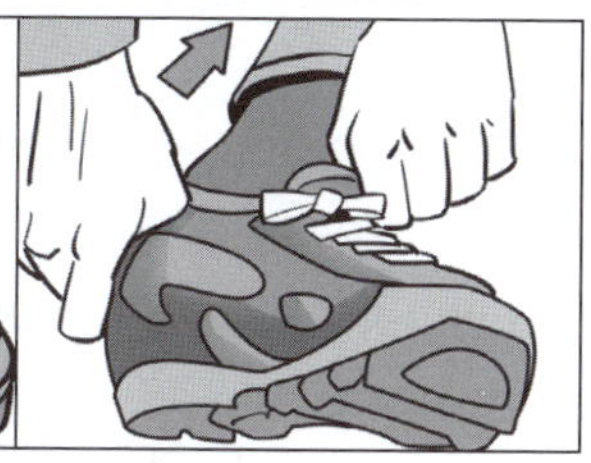

3 put on

4 give in

5 give out

2 ★★ **Complete the sentences. Use the verbs in box A with the words in box B.**

A give　give　give　pick　put　~~turn~~

B back　down　in　~~off~~　out　up

EXAM RULES

- *Turn off* all mobile phones during the exam.
- When teachers (**1**) give out the exam papers you can begin.
- At the end of the time, (**2**) put down your pens and (**3**) give in your papers immediately.
- If you drop anything on the floor, ask your teacher to (**4**) pick it up for you.
- If you borrow a calculator, please (**5**) give it back to your teacher at the end of the exam.

3 ★★ **Complete the sentences. Use the correct forms of the phrasal verbs in the box.**

give in　~~give up~~　give up　pick up
put on　take off　turn off

The boy *gave up* his chair when his grandmother walked into the room.

1 Give in your homework when you leave the classroom, please.

2 **Bev** I'm going to bed.
Jake OK. Turn off the lights downstairs, please.

3 Please don't leave your clothes on the floor. Pick them up and put them away!

4 Put on your jacket. It's cold outside.

5 Can you take off your shoes? I've just cleaned the floor.

6 My dad gave up smoking when he was 22.

4 ★★★ **Rewrite the sentences to replace the underlined words. Use *give* and the words in the box.**

away　back　out　~~up~~　up

My brother's going to <u>stop</u> eating chocolate for a month!
My brother's going to give up eating chocolate for a month!

1 Can you <u>return</u> my bike?
Can you give back my bike?

2 We should <u>stop trying to win</u> – they've beaten us!
We should give up – they've beaten us!

3 I'll <u>give</u> a lot of my CDs <u>to someone for nothing</u>.
I'll give away a lot of my CDs.

4 Our teacher <u>gives</u> the books <u>to everyone</u> at the beginning of the class.
Our teacher gives out the books at the beginning of the class.

Giving advice

1 ★ **Complete the dialogue. Use the words in the box.**

advice ~~ask~~ been dear must problem should think

Lola Can I *ask* your advice about something?
Max Sure. What's the (**1**) problem ?
Lola My best friend has (**2**) been really rude to me recently.
Max Oh, (**3**) dear . I think you (**4**) should speak to her about it.
Lola Do you (**5**) think I should find a new friend?
Max No, you (**6**) must speak to her first.
Lola OK. That's good (**7**) advice . Thanks.

2 ★★ **Answer the questions.**

Who's Lola asking for advice?
Max.

1 What's her problem?
Her best friend has been rude to her recently.

2 What's Max's advice?
Lola should speak to her friend about the problem.

3 What does Lola think is a possible solution?
Lola thinks she should find a new friend.

4 What does Lola think of Max's advice?
She thinks it's good advice.

3 ★★★ **Write a dialogue in your notebook like the dialogue in exercise 1. Use the ideas in the box.**

Problem: stressed about homework – too much to do **Advice**: organize time more carefully **Possible solution**: give up football **Advice**: ask your teacher to help you

Dictation

4 ★★ 4.09 **Listen. Listen again and write the sentences in your notebook.**

Essay: for and against

1 ★ **Complete the essay. Use the words in the box.**

Furthermore hand In On ~~one~~ opinion What

'We won't use traditional printed books in the future.' Do you agree or disagree?

On the *one* hand, traditional books are old-fashioned and expensive. (**1**) Furthermore , electronic books can do a lot more than traditional books. (**2**) On the other hand , it's easy to use traditional books. (**3**) What is more, you can use them anywhere. (**4**) In my opinion , we will use printed books and electronic books.

2 ★★ **Correct the mistakes.**

'The future will be more exciting than the present.' Do you agree or disagree?
On one hand, technology in the future will be amazing. *On the one hand*

1 It furthermore, will be really cheap.
Furthermore, it

2 On the another hand, problems such as global warming will be worse.
On the other hand

3 In conclusion, I'm believing the future will be more exciting. I believe

4 In me opinion, we will find solutions to our problems. In my opinion

3 ★★★ **Complete the essay.**

'Only governments can stop global warming.' Do you agree or disagree?

On the one hand, governments can change the price of petrol, electricity and gas. (**1**) Furthermore / What is more , they can make laws to change the amount of energy we use.

(**2**) On the other hand , if everyone tries to save energy, we will use less energy.

In conclusion, (**3**) I believe that we can all do something to stop global warming. (**4**) In my opinion , this is possible for everybody, including governments.

 Writing Builder page 109

9 Food and drink

Vocabulary

Food

1 ★ **Put the words in the box into groups.**

~~beef~~ carrots chicken mushrooms
peas peppers prawns tomato

Meat: beef, chicken

Vegetables: carrots, mushrooms, peas, peppers, tomato

Seafood: prawns

2 ★★ **Complete the words. Then match the words and the photos.**

b e e f

1 c h e e s e

2 s u s h i

3 c h i c k e n

4 c h i p s

5 p a s t a

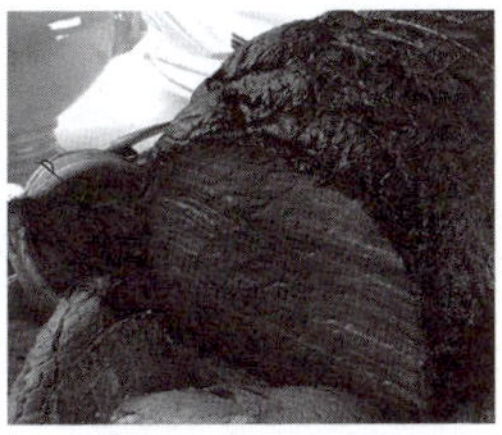

beef

c) chips

a) chicken

d) sushi

b) cheese

e) pasta

3 ★★ **Complete the chart. Use the words in exercise 2. Some words can go in more than one column.**

High in protein	High in carbohydrates	High in fat
beef	chips	beef
chicken	pasta	cheese
cheese	sushi	chicken
sushi		chips

4 ★★★ **Complete the sentences. Use your own ideas and the picture.**

My aunt makes *a wonderful dish with green beans and butter*.

1 I hate eating Students' answers ____________________.

2 I can cook ____________________.

3 My favourite Spanish dish is ____________________.

4 My favourite dish from another country is ____________________.

5 In my family, we eat a lot of ____________________.

6 In my family, we don't eat ____________________.

7 In Spain, people eat a lot of ____________________.

Present passive affirmative, negative and interrogative

1 ★ **Are these sentences active or passive? Write A or P.**

Brazil produces coffee. A

1 Is this ham from Spain? A
2 Millions of emails are sent every day. P
3 Sugar is used by the body to produce energy. P
4 Mexicans eat fish at Christmas. A
5 This T-shirt is cotton. A
6 Bananas aren't grown in Europe. P
7 Is this MP3 player sold in your country? P
8 Football is played all over the world. P

2 ★ **Choose the correct options.**

All our vegetables are **grew** / **grown** in our garden.

1 Our food **is** / **are** prepared by top-class chefs.
2 Takeaways **is** / **are** delivered to your home in less than fifteen minutes.
3 These toilets are **cleaned** / **clean** every hour.
4 These computers **is** / **are** turned off every night.
5 Our fish is **catch** / **caught** by dolphin-friendly fishing.

3 ★★ **Complete the text. Use the present passive of the verbs in brackets.**

In the UK, about 700,000 tonnes of chocolate *are eaten* (eat) every year. That's about fourteen kilograms per person! Over 200 different types of chocolate bar are sold (**1** sell) in British shops and over £100 million are spent (**2** spend) on advertising them. Chocolate is *very* popular. But how is it made (**3** make)?

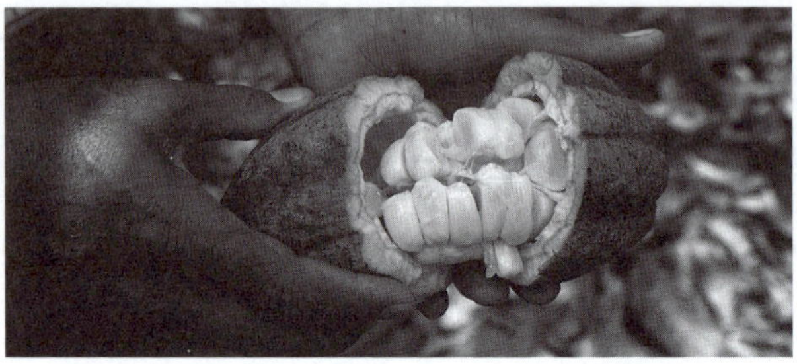

Chocolate is made (**4** make) from cocoa beans. They are found (**5** find) on cocoa trees, which are grown (**6** grow) in countries like the Ivory Coast and Ghana. The beans are dried (**7** dry) in the sun for seven days. Then they are sorted (**8** sort) into different qualities. The best beans are the most expensive.

In chocolate factories, the beans are cleaned (**9** clean) and cooked. Then they're crushed to make a substance called cocoa paste.

Sugar is added (**10** add) to make the cocoa paste sweet and the paste is mixed (**11** mix) with butter to make a liquid. When the liquid is cooled, it becomes hard and then you have ... chocolate!

Grammar Bank pages 82–83

4 ★★ **Write questions about the text in exercise 3.**

How much chocolate / eat / every year in the UK?
How much chocolate is eaten every year in the UK?

1 How many different types of chocolate bars / sell / in the UK?
How many different types of chocolate bars are sold in the UK?

2 How much / spend / on advertising chocolate?
How much is spent on advertising chocolate?

3 Where / cocoa beans / find?
Where are cocoa beans found?

4 Where / cocoa trees / grow?
Where are cocoa trees grown?

5 How long / the beans / dry for?
How long are the beans dried for?

6 What / the beans / sort / into?
What are the beans sorted into?

7 Why / sugar / add / to the beans?
Why is sugar added to the beans?

8 How / the liquid / make / hard?
How is the liquid made hard?

5 ★★ **Rewrite the active sentences. Use the passive.**

They don't teach Spanish at my school.
Spanish isn't taught at my school.

1 We don't serve alcohol here.
Alcohol isn't served here.

2 They don't speak Portuguese in Central American countries.
Portuguese isn't spoken in Central American countries.

3 They don't permit children to drive cars.
Children aren't permitted to drive cars.

4 They make sushi from fish and rice.
Sushi is made from fish and rice.

5 They don't grow oranges in England.
Oranges aren't grown in England.

6 ★★★ **Complete the dialogues. Use the active or the passive forms of the verbs in the boxes.**

be ~~come~~ eat make

Brad Where *does* cous cous *come* from?
Anna I think it (**1**) 's eaten mainly in Morocco.
Brad What (**2**) 's it made from?
Anna Wheat, I think. It (**3**) 's similar to pasta.

eat make mix sound

Brad How (**4**) 's haggis made?
Anna I think it's parts of a sheep which (**5**) are mixed with onion, herbs and salt.
Brad It (**6**) sounds horrible!
Anna It (**7**) 's eaten a lot in Scotland – on special days. I've never tried it.

7 ★★★ **Write passive sentences about the foods in box A. Use the verbs in box B.**

A

olives oranges paella Serrano ham ~~the best bread~~ the best seafood tortilla

B

~~bake~~ eat find grow make produce sell

The best bread in the world is baked by my grandmother.

1 Students' answers

2

3

4

5

6

1 **Do you eat healthily?**

Superfoods

All foods, even sweets, have *some* nutritional value. However, some foods are so good for you that they're known as 'superfoods'.

All fish is high in protein and vitamins. But **oily** fish, like salmon, is *very* good for you. If you eat lots of salmon, you'll have less chance of having heart problems. What's more, fish keeps your brain healthy!

The type of fat that's found in olive oil is good for your heart. However, olive oil has a lot of **calories**, so it gives you energy but makes you fat. A spoonful of olive oil has the same number of calories as a slice of bread and butter.

Blueberries contain lots of antioxidants. These are chemicals that protect you against heart disease and **cancer**. They're also good for your skin and are low in calories. However, most blueberries are **imported** into countries like England and Spain. So blueberries are good for you but importing them is bad for the environment!

Although 'superfoods' are very healthy, it's important to eat a **range** of foods. 'A handful of blueberries isn't enough to make you healthy,' says nutrition scientist Lucy Turnbull. 'Don't think about superfoods,' she says. 'Think about super **diets**!'

2 ★ **Read the text. Which three foods are 'superfoods'?**

Oily fish, olive oil and blueberries.

3 ★★ **Match the words and the definitions.**

oily *b)*

1 calories d)

2 cancer f)

3 import e)

4 range c)

5 diet a)

a) the type of food that someone usually eats

b) containing a lot of oil

c) different things of the same type

d) the amount of energy a food contains

e) bring something into your country from another country

f) a serious disease

4 ★★★ **Complete the summary.**

Superfoods are foods that are very *good* for you. One example is oily fish, like (**1**) salmon. It reduces your chance of (**2**) heart problems and is good for your (**3**) brain.

(**4**) Olive oil is another superfood. It is high in (**5**) calories but the type of (**6**) fat it contains is good for your heart.

(**7**) Blueberries are another example of a superfood. They're high in (**8**) antioxidants / chemicals, which protect your body from (**9**) heart disease and (**10**) cancer.

Superfoods are useful but it is best to have a balanced diet that includes lots of (**11**) different foods.

Partitives

1 ★ **Choose two correct options for each thing.**

a **packet** / **carton** / **bottle** of milk

1 a **can** / **slice** / **tube** of paint
2 a **bag** / **carton** / **box** of oranges
3 a **packet** / **box** / **slice** of pasta
4 a **spoonful** / **piece** / **bag** of sugar
5 a **tube** / **can** / **bottle** of lemonade

2 ★★ **Complete the phrases. Use the words in the box.**

bag	~~bottle~~	box	carton	jar	packet	piece	slice

a *bottle* of water

1 a carton of milk

2 a packet of chewing gum

3 a jar of olives

4 a piece of cake

5 a box of chocolates

6 a slice of bread

7 a bag of shopping

3 ★★ **Some of the partitives are wrong. Correct them.**

TILL RECEIPT

	ITEM	PRICE	
	a ~~bottle~~ of toothpaste	£1.00	*tube*
	a carton of orange juice	£1.20	✓
1	a packet of biscuits	£0.75	✓
2	a ~~bag~~ of jam	£1.10	jar
3	five ~~pieces~~ of bread	£2.50	slices
4	a ~~glass~~ of coffee	£1.20	cup
5	six cans of lemonade	£1.99	✓
6	a ~~tube~~ of matches	£0.25	box

4 ★★★ **Complete true sentences about your kitchen at home. Use partitives.**

In our kitchen there's / there are …

… *two packets of rice.*

1 Students' answers
2 ______
3 ______
4 ______
5 ______
6 ______
7 ______
8 ______

5 ★★★ **Write five things that you need to buy. Use partitives.**

Some cans of cola.

1 Students' answers
2 ______
3 ______
4 ______
5 ______

In a café

1 ★ **Put the sentences in the correct order.**

Waiter	I'll bring the food to your table. 9
Waiter	Good afternoon. Can I help you? 1
Waiter	A chicken salad and a glass of apple juice. That's £8.00, please. 5
Waiter	Certainly. Anything to drink? 3
Waiter	£20.00. Thank you … Here's your change. 7
Jess	Thank you. 8
Jess	Yes. Could I have a glass of apple juice, please? 4
Jess	I'd like a chicken salad, please. 2
Jess	Here you are. 6

2 ★★ **Answer the questions.**

Is Jess ordering lunch or breakfast?
She's ordering lunch.

1 What food does she order?
She orders a chicken salad.

2 What drink does she order?
She orders a glass of apple juice.

3 How much is the food?
It's £8.00.

4 How much money does Jess give the waiter?
She gives him £20.00.

3 ★★★ **Write a dialogue in your notebook like the dialogue in exercise 1. Use the menu.**

FOOD	
Moussaka	£8.00
Tortilla	£7.50
Prawn curry	£9.00
Chicken salad	£6.50
DRINKS	
Coffee / tea	£1.80
Orange / apple juice	£1.50
Cola / lemonade	£1.50

Dictation

4 ★★ 4.10 **Listen. Listen again and write the sentences in your notebook.**

Describing your best meal

1 ★ **Choose the correct options.**

a) Who had dessert.
(b)) Who had dessert?

1 a) It's necesary to book a table.
(b)) It's necessary to book a table.

2 (a)) Where did you eat?
b) Where you ate?

3 (a)) We often eat out together.
b) Often we eat out together.

4 a) I've forgoten what we ate.
(b)) I've forgotten what we ate.

2 ★★ **Correct the mistakes.**

The meal was ~~on~~ July. *in*

1 The food was ~~french~~. French

2 ~~I~~ already ordered. I've

3 The food was really ~~diferent~~. different

4 If ~~I'll~~ get a salad, ~~I~~ share it with you.
I , I'll

5 ~~¡~~The meal was fantastic! The

6 Everyone was ~~shoutting~~ and having a great time. shouting

7 My friend ~~was having~~ steak but I don't eat meat. had

3 ★★★ **Read the description of Jerry's best meal. Correct the mistakes.**

The best meal I've ever ~~have~~ was a meal with friends last year. We ~~celebrated~~ the end of the school year. It was a ~~friday~~ night and we went to a tapas restaurant.

~~We've ordered~~ about twenty ~~diferent~~ dishes to share so there was ~~quiet~~ a lot of food! My favourites ~~was~~ the seafood and the tortilla. ~~everyone~~ was chatting happily about ~~there~~ plans for the holidays. For dessert I had a fruit salad and my best friend, Carl, tried some ~~cheese Spanish~~. It was delicious.

had	5 quite
1 were celebrating	6 were
2 Friday	7 Everyone
3 We ordered	8 their
4 different	9 Spanish cheese

Writing Builder page 110

be and *have got*: present simple

be: present simple

Afirmativa		Formas contractas
I	am	I'm
he / she / it	is	he's / she's / it's
you / we / they	are	you're / we're / they're

Forma afirmativa: sujeto + *am / is / are*.

I'm from Manchester. Soy de Manchester.

Negativa		Formas contractas	
I	am not	I'm	not
he / she / it	is not	he / she / it	isn't
you / we / they	are not	you / we / they	aren't

Forma negativa: sujeto + *am / is / are* + *not*.

Al hablar se suelen utilizar las formas contractas.

She isn't at home. No está en casa.

Interrogativa	Respuestas breves	
	Afirmativa	Negativa
Am I...?	Yes, I am.	No, I'm not.
Is he / she / it ...?	Yes, he / she / it is.	No, he / she / it isn't.
Are you / we / they ...?	Yes, you / we / they are.	No, you / we / they aren't.

Forma interrogativa: *am / is / are* + sujeto.

El signo de interrogación se coloca sólo al final de la frase.

Is Beckham from London? ¿Beckham es de Londres?

En las respuestas breves afirmativas no se utilizan las formas contractas; por el contrario, en las respuestas breves negativas es más frecuente utilizar las formas contractas.

'Are you angry?' 'Yes, I am.' (NO ~~'Yes, I'm.'~~) "¿Estás enfadado?" "Sí."
'Are you sad?' 'No, I'm not.' "¿Estás triste?" "No."

El signo de interrogación se coloca al final de la frase.

Usos

El verbo *be* se traduce por "ser" o "estar", y también por "tener" con ciertas expresiones.

My favourite subject is IT. Mi asignatura preferida es informática.
I'm in the class. Estoy en la clase.
Kevin is sixteen years old. Kevin tiene dieciséis años.

! ¡Ojo!

Con ciertas expresiones se debe utilizar el verbo *be*, y no *have*.

I'm 13. (NO ~~I have 13.~~) Tengo 13 años.
I'm hungry. (NO ~~I have hungry.~~) Tengo hambre.
I'm hot. (NO ~~I have hot.~~) Tengo calor.

have got: present simple

Afirmativa		Formas contractas
I / you / we / they	have got	I've / you've / we've / they've got
he / she / it	has got	he's / she's / it's got

Forma afirmativa: sujeto + *have / has got* + objeto directo.

En la tercera persona del singular, *have got* se convierte en *has got*.

Negativa		Formas contractas
I / you / we / they	have not got	I / you / we / they haven't got
he / she / it	has not got	he / she / it hasn't got

La negativa se forma colocando *not* detrás de *have* y *has*. Se suelen utilizar las formas contractas.

Charlie hasn't got any brothers or sisters. Charlie no tiene hermanos.

Interrogativa		
Have	I / you / we / they	got...?
Has	he / she / it	got...?

Forma interrogativa: *Have / Has* + sujeto + *got* + objeto directo. En la interrogativa no se utilizan las formas contractas de *have / has*.

Has Anna got a sister? ¿Anna tiene una hermana?

Respuestas breves					
Afirmativa			Negativa		
Yes,	I / you / we / they	have.	No,	I / you / we / they	haven't.
Yes,	he / she / it	has.	No,	he / she / it	hasn't.

En las respuestas breves afirmativas no se utilizan las formas contractas; por el contrario, en las respuestas breves negativas es más frecuente utilizar las formas contractas.

'Has she got dark hair?' 'Yes, she has.' (NO ~~'Yes, she's.'~~) "¿Tiene el pelo moreno?" "Sí."
'Have you got a car?' 'No, I haven't.' "¿Tienes coche?" "No."

Usos

Have got significa "tener", y se utiliza para expresar posesión.

I've got a new bike. Tengo una bicicleta nueva.

Have got también se utiliza para describir el aspecto físico de las personas.

'Has he got blue eyes?' 'No, he hasn't.' "¿Tiene los ojos azules?" "No."

! ¡Ojo!

En las respuestas breves no se utiliza *got*.

'Have you got a dictionary?' 'Yes, I have.'
(NO ~~'Yes, I have got.'~~) "¿Tienes un diccionario?" "Sí."

En la forma interrogativa de *have got* no se utiliza el auxiliar *do / does*.

Have you got a computer? (NO ~~Do you have got a computer?~~)
¿Tienes un ordenador?

can / can't

La forma *can* es la misma para todas las personas: *I can, you can, he / she / it can, we can, you can, they can.*

Forma afirmativa: sujeto + *can* + infinitivo del verbo sin *to*.

I can play the piano. Yo sé tocar el piano.

Forma negativa: sujeto + *can't* + infinitivo del verbo sin *to*.

En la negativa es más normal utilizar la forma contracta.

I can't meet you tonight. No puedo quedar contigo esta noche.

Forma interrogativa: *Can* + sujeto + infinitivo del verbo sin *to*.

Can you ski? ¿Sabes esquiar?

Con el verbo *can* nunca se utiliza un auxiliar para formar la negativa o la interrogativa.

I can't ride a bike. (NO ~~I don't ride a bike.~~) No sé andar en bici.
Can he cook? (NO ~~Does he can cook?~~) ¿Sabe cocinar?

En las respuestas breves negativas se suele utilizar la forma contracta.

'Can your brother play chess?' 'Yes, he can.' / 'No, he can't.' "¿Tu hermano sabe jugar al ajedrez?" "Sí." / "No."

Usos

Can se utiliza para expresar capacidades, posibilidades y habilidades. Se traduce por "poder" o "saber".

I can't open the window! ¡No puedo abrir la ventana!
Can he play football? ¿Sabe jugar al fútbol?

En frases interrogativas y respuestas breves, *can* también se utiliza para pedir y dar permiso.

'Can I use your mobile phone?' 'Yes, you can.' / 'No, you can't.' "¿Puedo usar tu teléfono móvil?" "Sí." / "No."

Present continuous

Afirmativa			Formas contractas	
I	am	reading	I'm	reading
he / she / it	is	reading	he's / she's / it's	reading
you / we / they	are	reading	you're / we're / they're	reading

Forma afirmativa: sujeto + *present simple* del verbo *be* + forma en *-ing* del verbo principal.

I'm eating a banana. Estoy comiendo un plátano.

Negativa			Formas contractas	
I	am not	reading	I'm not	reading
he / she / it	is not	reading	he's / she's / it's not	reading
you / we / they	are not	reading	you / we / they aren't	reading

Forma negativa: sujeto + negativa del verbo *be* + forma en *-ing* del verbo principal.

Hay dos contracciones posibles. Ambas se utilizan indistintamente.

She isn't reading her magazine. She's not reading her magazine. No está leyendo su revista.

Interrogativa		
Am	I	reading?
Is	he / she / it	reading?
Are	you / we / they	reading?

Forma interrogativa: *Am / Is / Are* + sujeto + forma en *-ing* del verbo principal.

Respuestas breves					
Afirmativa			Negativa		
Yes,	I	am.	No,	I'm	not.
Yes,	he / she / it	is.	No,	he / she / it	isn't.
Yes,	you / we / they	are.	No,	you / we / they	aren't.

En las respuestas breves afirmativas no se utilizan las formas contractas.

'Are you studying?' 'Yes, I am.' (NO ~~'Yes, I'm.'~~) "¿Estás estudiando?" "Sí."
En la forma negativa de las respuestas breves se pueden utilizar ambas contracciones indistintamente.
'Is he playing basketball?' 'No, he isn't. / No, he's not.' "¿Está jugando al baloncesto?" "No."

En la forma *I am* no se puede utilizar la contracción con *-n't*.

I'm not playing. (NO ~~I amn't playing.~~) No estoy jugando.

Spelling rules: *-ing* form

1 Con la mayoría de los verbos, se añade *-ing* al infinitivo sin *to*.
eat / eating speak / speaking

2 Los verbos acabados en una *-e* muda pierden la *-e* antes de añadir *-ing*.
write / writing dance / dancing

3 En los monosílabos acabados en una consonante precedida de una sola vocal, la consonante se duplica y se añade *-ing*.
run / running chat / chatting

4 Los verbos que terminan en *-y* no duplican la consonante final.
play / playing

be and *have got*: present simple

1 Complete Robert's email. Use *be* and *have got* affirmative or negative.

Hi, my name is Robert Greaves. I (**1**) 'm fifteen years old. I (**2**) 'm from London. I (**3**) 've got a little sister. I (**4**) haven't got any brothers. My favourite sports (**5**) are football and ice skating.

My best friend is David Thomson. He (**6**) isn't fifteen: he's sixteen. He (**7**) hasn't got any brothers or sisters.

I'm going now – I (**8**) 'm really hungry!

2 Read the email in exercise 1 again. Write questions and answers about Robert. Use *be* and *have got*.

How old is Robert?
He's fifteen.

1 Has he got any brothers and sisters?
He's got a little sister. He hasn't got any brothers.

2 What are his favourite sports?
His favourite sports are football and ice skating.

3 Who is his best friend?
His best friend is David Thomson.

4 Is Robert hungry?
Yes, he is.

3 Put the words in the correct order to make questions. Use *be* and *have got*. Then write true answers.

from / are / where / you / ?
Where are you from?
I'm from America.

1 sisters / you / any / have / brothers / and / got / ?
Have you got any brothers and sisters?
Students' answers

2 you / or / are / hungry / thirsty / ?
Are you hungry or thirsty?

3 mother / has / hair / got / your / dark / ?
Has your mother got dark hair?

can / can't

4 Write questions and answers about Tim. Use *can* and *can't*.

cook a Spanish tortilla? ✓
Can he cook a Spanish tortilla? Yes, he can.

1 run 100 kilometres? ✗
Can he run 100 kilometres? No, he can't.

2 play the guitar? ✓
Can he play the guitar? Yes, he can.

3 ski? ✗
Can he ski? No, he can't.

Present continuous

5 Complete the paragraph. Use the present continuous forms of the verbs in brackets.

Emma is sitting (sit) in an Internet café after school. It 's raining (**1** rain). She 's wearing (**2** wear) jeans and a jumper. She isn't doing (**3** not do) her homework. She 's eating (**4** eat) a sandwich and she 's talking (**5** talk) to a boy with short, fair hair. They 're chatting (**6** chat) about their favourite films.

6 Read the paragraph in exercise 5 again. Write questions about Emma and her friend. Use the present continuous. Then write the answers.

Emma / sit / at home ?
Is Emma sitting at home? No, she isn't.

1 it / rain ?
Is it raining? Yes, it is.

2 Emma / eat / a sandwich ?
Is Emma eating a sandwich? Yes, she is.

3 Emma and her friend / chat / about music ?
Are Emma and her friend chatting about music?
No, they aren't.

7 Complete the dialogue. Use the present continuous.

Ann Hi, Jo. Are you doing (you do) anything?
Jo Not really. I 'm reading (**1** read) a book. What are you doing (**2** you do)?
Ann Well, I 'm having (**3** have) a meal with friends. Do you want to come?
Jo Thanks, Ann, but I'm tired and I 'm going (**4** go) to bed early. Sorry.

Present simple

Afirmativa	
I / you / we / they	play
he /she / it	plays

Forma afirmativa: sujeto + verbo.

I like sport. Me gusta el deporte.

Negativa	Formas contractas
I / you / we / they do not watch	I / you / we / they don't watch
he / she / it does not watch	he / she / it doesn't watch

Forma negativa: sujeto + *don't* / *doesn't* + infinitivo sin *to*.

Robert doesn't play basketball. Robert no juega al baloncesto.

Interrogativa
Do I / you / we / they teach?
Does he / she / it teach?

Forma interrogativa: *Do* / *Does* + sujeto + infinitivo sin *to*.

Does Lisa like chess? ¿A Lisa le gusta el ajedrez?

Respuestas breves	
Afirmativa	**Negativa**
Yes, I / you / we / they do.	No, I / you / we / they don't.
Yes, he / she / it does.	No, he / she / it doesn't.

En las respuestas breves afirmativas, *do* / *does* sigue al pronombre sujeto.

En la negativa se utilizan las formas contractas *don't* / *doesn't*.

'Do you listen to music every day?' 'Yes, I do.' / 'No, I don't.'
"¿Escuchas música todos los días?" "Sí." / "No."

! ¡Ojo!

En las formas negativa e interrogativa, el verbo principal no lleva *-s* en la 3ª persona del singular.

Tom doesn't play tennis. (NO ~~Tom doesn't plays tennis.~~) Tom no juega al tenis.

Spelling rules: 3rd person singular

1 La forma de la 3ª persona del singular (*he / she / it*) siempre termina en *-s*.
He plays football. Juega al fútbol.

2 Los verbos que terminan en consonante + *-y* cambian la *-y* por *-ies*.
She studies French. Estudia francés.
Si el verbo termina en vocal + *-y*, solo se añade *-s*.
play / plays buy / buys

3 Si el verbo termina en *-s*, *-ch*, *-sh*, *-x*, *-o*, *-z*, se añade *-es*.
watch / watches go / goes

4 El verbo *have* es un verbo irregular.
Kelly has a good camera. Kelly tiene una cámara de fotos buena.

Usos

Explicar cosas que suceden habitualmente y describir rutinas de todos los días, todas las semanas, etc.

I watch TV every day. Veo la tele a diario.

Expresar verdades generales y definiciones.

Paris is the capital of France. París es la capital de Francia.

Indicar gustos, opiniones y sentimientos.

I like photography. Me gusta la fotografía.

Adverbs of frequency

0% never — hardly ever — sometimes — often — usually — 100% always

Usos

Los adverbios de frecuencia se colocan delante del verbo principal.

We usually go to the shopping centre on Saturday. Normalmente vamos al centro comercial los sábados.

He doesn't always walk to school. No siempre va andando al colegio.

Do you often go out with friends? ¿Salís a menudo con amigos?

En el caso del verbo *be*, se colocan detrás.

My sister is never at home. Mi hermana nunca está en casa.

Present tense contrast

El *present continuous* indica que una acción está ocurriendo mientras se habla. A menudo va acompañado de expresiones como *now* (ahora), *at the moment* (en este momento) y *today* (hoy).

'What are you doing?' 'I'm reading a magazine.' (NO ~~'What do you do?'~~) "¿Qué haces?" "Estoy leyendo una revista."
At the moment, I'm drawing. En este momento estoy dibujando.

El *present simple* indica que una acción ocurre habitualmente o con regularidad.

It often rains in September. A menudo llueve en septiembre.

Los verbos que expresan sentimientos y procesos mentales se suelen utilizar en la forma simple, no en la forma continua.

Son verbos como *understand* (entender), *know* (saber), *remember* (recordar), *like* (gustar), *love* (amar), *hate* (odiar) y *want* (querer).

I hate dogs. (NO ~~I'm hating dogs.~~) Odio los perros.
I don't know. (NO ~~I'm not knowing.~~) No lo sé.

! ¡Ojo!

Para hablar de algo que está ocurriendo en este momento, se debe utilizar el *present continuous*, nunca el *present simple*.

'Where are you going?' 'I'm going to the sports centre.' (NO ~~'Where do you go?' 'I go to the sports centre.'~~) "¿Adónde vas?" "Voy al polideportivo."
'What does your father do?' 'He's a doctor.' "¿A qué se dedica tu padre?" "Es médico."
'What's your sister doing?' 'She's watching TV.' "¿Qué está haciendo tu hermana?" "Está viendo la tele."

Present simple

1 Complete the sentences. Use the present simple forms of the verbs in the box.

collect go ~~listen~~ not like not speak not watch play study

Simon listens to his MP3 player all day.

1 Andy collects stamps.
2 Paul always goes jogging in the morning.
3 My sister plays computer games every evening.
4 I don't like cooking – it's boring!
5 David doesn't watch TV after school.
6 Jackie studies very hard for all her exams.
7 Terence doesn't speak Spanish – only English.

2 Write questions. Use the present simple interrogative. Then write short answers.

Carol / read / fashion magazines? ✓
Does Carol read fashion magazines?
Yes, she does.

1 Joe and his friends / play basketball? ✗
Do Joe and his friends play basketball?
No, they don't.

2 Susie / go shopping / with friends? ✗
Does Susie go shopping with friends?
No, she doesn't.

3 Susie and Ann / have lunch / at school? ✓
Do Susie and Ann have lunch at school?
Yes, they do.

4 Ann / visit / chat rooms / every day? ✗
Does Ann visit chat rooms every day?
No, she doesn't.

5 Harry / take / good photos? ✓
Does Harry take good photos?
Yes, he does.

3 Write questions. Use the present simple interrogative. Then write true answers.

How / you travel home from school?
How do you travel home from school?
By bus.

1 What time / you do your homework?
What time do you do your homework?
Students' answers

2 What / you eat in the evening?
What do you eat in the evening?

3 Where / you have lunch?
Where do you have lunch?

4 Who / you talk to in the evening?
Who do you talk to in the evening?

5 When / you go to bed?
When do you go to bed?

Adverbs of frequency

4 Complete the text. Use the present simple and put the adverbs in the correct positions.

Ben usually gets up (usually / get up) at eight o'clock, but he is sometimes (**1** sometimes / be) late. He often has (**2** often / have) toast for breakfast, but he hardly ever drinks (**3** hardly ever / drink) tea. He always catches (**4** always / catch) the bus to school with his sister, Linda. They never cycle (**5** never / cycle) to school – they 're always (**6** always / be) too tired in the morning!

Present tense contrast

5 Choose the correct options.

Jo never **wears** / **is wearing** jeans to school.

1 We **don't understand** / **aren't understanding** German.
2 Oh, no! It **snows** / **'s snowing** again!
3 'Hi, Leo! Where **do you go** / **are you going**?' 'Home.'
4 I **don't think** / **'m not thinking** that's a nice T-shirt.
5 Look! John **chats** / **'s chatting** to Jenny!

Past simple

Afirmativa
I / you / he / she / it / we / you / they watched

Forma afirmativa: sujeto + infinitivo del verbo sin *to* + *ed*.

Algunos verbos tienen formas regulares de pasado, y otros tienen formas irregulares. La forma afirmativa del pasado regular es la misma para todas las personas.

Los verbos irregulares no siguen reglas ortográficas establecidas. Tendrás que aprendértelos de memoria en el apartado de verbos irregulares que aparece al final del libro.

go / went see / saw drink / drank have / had

Recuerda que la forma verbal de los verbos irregulares también es la misma para las distintas personas del verbo: *I went, you went, he / she / it went, we went, you went, they went.*

Consulta la lista de verbos irregulares en el interior de la contraportada.

Negativa	Formas contractas
I / you / he / she / it / we / you / they did not go	I / you / he / she / it / we / you / they didn't go

Forma negativa: sujeto + *didn't* + infinitivo del verbo sin *to*.

En las frases negativas se suele utilizar la forma contracta.

He didn't finish his breakfast. No acabó de desayunar.

Interrogativa	Respuestas breves	
	Afirmativa	Negativa
Did I / you / he / she / it / we / you / they leave?	Yes, I / you / he / she / it / we / you / they did.	No, I / you / he / she / it / we / you / they didn't.

Forma interrogativa: *Did* + sujeto + infinitivo del verbo sin *to*.

Did Greg phone you? ¿Greg te llamó?

En la forma negativa de las respuestas breves se suele utilizar la forma contracta.

'Did you send an email to Melissa?' 'Yes, I did.' 'No, I didn't.' "¿Le enviaste un email a Melissa?" "Sí." / "No."

Recuerda que en las frases negativas e interrogativas, y también en las respuestas breves, el verbo auxiliar es el mismo para todas las personas (*did / didn't*).

Además, en las frases negativas e interrogativas, el infinitivo del verbo sin *to* se mantiene invariable, tanto en los verbos regulares como en los irregulares.

We didn't eat at the party. No comimos en la fiesta.
Did she go late? ¿Se marchó tarde?

Spelling rules: past simple (regular verbs)

1 Con la mayoría de los verbos, se añade *-ed* al infinitivo del verbo sin *to*.
listen / listened work / worked

2 Si el verbo acaba en una *-e* muda, se añade *-d*.
like / liked arrive / arrived

3 Si acaba en consonante + *y*, la *y* se transforma en *i* y se añade *-ed*.
worry / worried study / studied

4 Si el verbo acaba en una vocal y una consonante, la consonante final se duplica y se añade *-ed*.
stop / stopped chat / chatted

5 Los verbos que terminan en *-y* no duplican la consonante final.
play / played

Usos

El *past simple* se utiliza para hablar de acciones que ocurrieron en un momento determinado del pasado. Las expresiones de tiempo fijan la acción en un momento concreto.

could / couldn't

La forma *could* es la misma para todas las personas: *I / you / he / she / it / we / you / they could.*

Forma afirmativa: sujeto + *could* + infinitivo del verbo sin *to*.

I could read when I was three. A los tres años ya sabía leer.

Forma negativa: sujeto + *couldn't* + infinitivo del verbo sin *to*.

En la negativa es más frecuente utilizar las formas contractas.

Sarah couldn't go to the party. Sarah no pudo ir a la fiesta.

Forma interrogativa: *Could* + sujeto + infinitivo del verbo sin *to*.

Las respuestas breves afirmativas se forman con el pronombre sujeto seguido de *could*.

En la forma negativa se utiliza el pronombre sujeto seguido de *couldn't*.

'Could you talk when you were two?' 'Yes, I could.' / 'No, I couldn't.' "¿Sabías hablar a los dos años?" "Sí." / "No."

Usos

Could y *couldn't* son las formas de pasado de *can* y *can't*. Expresan la capacidad de hacer algo en el pasado, y se traducen por "poder / no poder" o "saber / no saber".

I could swim when I was two. Con dos años ya sabía nadar.
I couldn't sleep yesterday. Ayer no pude dormir.

Past simple of be: *was / were*

Afirmativa
I / he / she / it was
we / you / they were

Forma afirmativa: sujeto + *was / were*.

I was at home last night. Anoche estuve en casa.

Negativa	Forma contracta
I / he / she / it was not	I / he / she / it wasn't
we / you / they were not	we / you / they weren't

Forma negativa: sujeto + *was / were* + *not*.

I wasn't at school. No estaba en el colegio.

Interrogativa	Respuestas breves	
	Afirmativa	Negativa
Was I / he / she / it...?	Yes, I / he / she / it was.	No, I / he / she / it wasn't.
Were we / you / they...?	Yes, we / you / they were.	No, we / you / they weren't.

Forma interrogativa: *Was / Were* + sujeto.

Were you nervous? ¿Estabas nerviosa?

En las respuestas breves negativas se suelen utilizar las formas contractas.

'Were you tired?' 'Yes, I was.' / 'No, I wasn't.' "¿Estabas cansada?" "Sí." / "No."

Usos

Was y *were* son las formas de pasado del verbo *be*.

Kevin was in Manchester. Kevin estaba en Manchester.
We were thirsty. Teníamos sed.

Past simple

1 Write the past simple forms of the verbs.

miss missed
1 invite invited
2 accept accepted
3 stop stopped
4 study studied
5 tidy tidied
6 watch watched
7 arrive arrived

2 Write the base forms of the verbs.

fell fall
1 got get
2 left leave
3 made make
4 took take
5 did do
6 found find
7 spoke speak

3 Complete the text. Use the past simple affirmative forms of the verbs in the box.

buy come give go send spend stay travel ~~win~~

Last year my brother **won** the lottery. He (1) bought a new car for my parents. He (2) gave me a computer. Then he (3) went on holiday. He (4) travelled around the world and (5) stayed in very expensive hotels. He (6) sent us emails every week. He (7) spent all the money but he (8) came home happy.

4 Complete the text. Use the past simple negative.

I **didn't win** (win) the lottery last year and I didn't buy (1 buy) presents for my family. I didn't go (2 go) on holiday and I didn't travel (3 travel) around the world.

5 Write questions and short answers about Sarah's holiday. Use the past simple affirmative (✓) and negative (✗).

went to Italy? ✓
Did Sarah go to Italy?
Yes, she did.

1 climbed the Statue of Liberty? ✗
Did Sarah climb the Statue of Liberty?
No, she didn't.

2 ate in cheap restaurants? ✓
Did Sarah eat in cheap restaurants?
Yes, she did.

3 saw Buckingham Palace? ✗
Did Sarah see Buckingham Palace?
No, she didn't.

4 visited lots of museums? ✓
Did Sarah visit lots of museums?
Yes, she did.

6 Put the words in the correct order.

dinner / last night / where / have / you / did / ?
Where did you have dinner last night?

1 on Saturday evening / you / were / where / ?
Where were you on Saturday evening?

2 eat / who / yesterday / with / you / did / ?
Who did you eat with yesterday?

3 did / breakfast / time / this morning / what / you / have / ?
What time did you have breakfast this morning?

could / couldn't

7 Complete the sentences. Use *can*, *can't*, *could* or *couldn't* and the verbs in the box.

finish go ~~open~~ play

We **can't open** the door. We haven't got a key.

1 I could play chess when I was four! My mum taught me.

2 Dinner time! You can finish your homework later.

3 She couldn't go to school last week. She had flu.

Past simple of *be*: *was / were*

8 Complete the sentences. Use *was*, *wasn't*, *were*, *weren't*.

1 Mark said the match **was** boring because there weren't any good players, but I wasn't bored.

2 'Was he pleased with his maths mark?' 'No, he wasn't!'

3 'You weren't at home last night.' 'Yes, I was!'

4 'Were the groups at the concert good?' 'No, they were terrible!'

Past continuous

Afirmativa
I was laughing
he / she / it was laughing
we / you / they were laughing

Forma afirmativa: sujeto + *was / were* + forma en *-ing* del verbo principal.

Last night I was reading a book. Anoche estuve leyendo un libro.

Negativa		Formas contractas	
I	was not laughing	I	wasn't laughing
he /she / it	was not laughing	he / she / it	wasn't laughing
we / you / they	were not laughing	we / you / they	weren't laughing

Forma negativa: sujeto + *was / were* + *not* + forma en *-ing* del verbo principal.

I wasn't sleeping. No estaba durmiendo.

Interrogativa	Respuestas breves	
	Afirmativa	Negativa
Was I laughing?	Yes, I was.	No, I wasn't.
Was he / she / it laughing?	Yes, he / she / it was.	No, he / she / it wasn't.
Were we / you / they laughing?	Yes, we / you / they were.	No, we / you / they weren't.

Forma interrogativa: *Was / Were* + sujeto + forma en *-ing* del verbo principal.

Were you watching a film ? ¿Estabas viendo una película?

En las respuestas breves negativas se suelen utilizar las formas contractas.

'Were you laughing?' 'Yes, I was.' / 'No, I wasn't.' "¿Te estabas riendo?" "Sí." / "No."

Usos

El *past continuous* se utiliza para hablar de algo que estaba ocurriendo en un momento determinado del pasado.

At eight o'clock yesterday evening I was listening to music. Ayer a las ocho de la tarde estaba escuchando música.

Este tiempo verbal también se utiliza para referirse a una acción prolongada que tuvo lugar en el pasado.

I was studying all day on Sunday. El domingo me pasé todo el día estudiando.

Past simple and past continuous

A menudo utilizamos el *past simple* con el *past continuous* para describir una acción breve que sucedió mientras se estaba desarrollando otra más larga.

I was looking at the magazines when I saw Helen. Estaba mirando las revistas cuando vi a Helen.
As we were going home, I looked at Helen. Mientras íbamos para casa, miré a Helen.

Adverbs

La mayoría de los adverbios se forman añadiendo *-ly*.

Al adjetivo:

quick / quickly bad / badly slow / slowly careful / carefully

Los adjetivos que terminan en *-y* cambian la *-y* por *-i*.

noisy / noisily funny / funnily pretty / prettily happy / happily

El adverbio derivado de *good* es *well*.

He sings very well. Canta muy bien.

Algunos adjetivos y adverbios presentan formas idénticas.

late / late early / early fast / fast

Past continuous

1 Write affirmative and negative sentences about what was happening at ten o'clock. Use the past continuous.

Jim and Adela go to the sports centre. / They not go to the cinema.
Jim and Adela were going to the sports centre. They weren't going to the cinema.

1 Allie wear jeans. / She not wear a skirt.
Allie was wearing jeans. She wasn't wearing a skirt.

2 Sam sit in the garden. / He not sit in the living room.
Sam was sitting in the garden. He wasn't sitting in the living room.

3 They play football. / They not go shopping.
They were playing football. They weren't going shopping.

4 Kate run. / She not cycle.
Kate was running. She wasn't cycling.

5 It snow. / It not rain.
It was snowing. It wasn't raining.

6 Andrea carry a book. / She not carry a bag.
Andrea was carrying a book. She wasn't carrying a bag.

7 They speak Spanish. / They not speak German.
They were speaking Spanish. They weren't speaking German.

2 Complete the paragraph. Use the past continuous forms of the verbs in the box.

film	listen	not do	~~not talk~~
play	read	smile	watch

Yesterday evening at nine o'clock I was at home with my family. The room was quiet – we **weren't talking** to each other. My dad (**1**) was reading a magazine. My mum (**2**) was watching TV. She (**3**) was smiling – it was a comedy programme. My sister (**4**) was listening to her MP3 player, and my two brothers (**5**) were playing computer games. I (**6**) wasn't doing any of these things. I (**7**) was filming them with my mobile phone!

3 Put the words in the correct order to write questions. Then write true answers.

having / at 7:30 this morning / a shower / you / were / ?
Were you having a shower at 7:30 this morning?
Yes, I was. / No, I wasn't. I was having breakfast.

1 at eight o'clock last night / playing / were / computer games / you / ?
Were you playing computer games at eight o'clock last night?
Students' answers

2 it / was / in your town / raining / yesterday / ?
Was it raining in your town yesterday?

3 shining / at 10:30 this morning / the sun / was / ?
Was the sun shining at 10:30 this morning?

4 trainers / wearing / you / yesterday / were / ?
Were you wearing trainers yesterday?

5 were / sleeping / at 10 a.m. on Sunday / you / ?
Were you sleeping at 10 a.m. on Sunday?

Adverbs

4 Write the adverbs.

	slow	*slowly*	4	good	well
1	careful	carefully	5	lucky	luckily
2	fast	quickly	6	hard	hard
3	bad	badly	7	late	late

5 Complete the sentences. Use some of the adjectives and adverbs from exercise 4.

Please drive **slowly**! You're going too fast.

1 Please, hold these glasses carefully! They're very expensive.

2 Are you French? You speak French very well!

3 I forgot my keys at home. Luckily, a window was open!

4 Shh! Be careful! Everyone is asleep.

have to

Afirmativa	
I / you / we / they	have to help
he / she / it	has to help

Forma afirmativa: sujeto + *have* / *has to* + infinitivo.
Ed has to help his mother. Ed tiene que ayudar a su madre.

Negativa	
I / you / we / they	don't have to help
he / she / it	doesn't have to help

Forma negativa: sujeto + *don't* / *doesn't* + *have to* + infinitivo.
Charlie doesn't have to do the ironing. Charlie no tiene que planchar.

Interrogativa	Respuestas breves	
	Afirmativa	Negativa
Do I / we / you / they have to help?	Yes, I / we / you / they do.	No, I / we / you / they don't.
Does he / she / it have to help?	Yes, he / she / it does.	No, he / she / it doesn't.

Forma interrogativa: *Do* / *Does* + sujeto + *have to* + infinitivo.
Do you have to help with the housework? ¿Tienes que ayudar con las tareas de la casa?

En las respuestas breves negativas se suelen utilizar las formas contractas.

'Does he have to leave?' 'Yes, he does.' / 'No, he doesn't.' "¿Tiene que irse?" "Sí." / "No."

Usos

Have to expresa la obligación o la necesidad de hacer algo.
I have to look after my sister tonight. Esta noche tengo que cuidar a mi hermana.

Don't have to indica que no hay obligación de hacer algo.
I don't have to get up for school tomorrow. Mañana no tengo que levantarme para ir al instituto.
Charlie doesn't have to make his bed. Charlie no tiene que hacer su cama.

some and *any*

Some y *any* se utilizan con sustantivos tanto contables como incontables.
There's some fish for dinner. Hay pescado para cenar.
There aren't any pens. No hay ningún bolígrafo.

Some se utiliza en frases afirmativas.
I've got some bananas. Tengo unos plátanos.

Con los sustantivos en plural, *some* se traduce por "unos / unas / algunos / algunas", mientras que su traducción es "un poco de / algo de" con los sustantivos incontables.
She's got some books. Tiene unos / algunos libros.
Is there any lemonade? ¿Hay (algo de) limonada?

Sustantivos incontables	Sustantivos contables
There's some milk.	There are some biscuits.
There isn't any milk	There aren't any biscuits
Is there any milk?	Are there any biscuits?

En las oraciones negativas e interrogativas se utiliza *any*.

En las oraciones negativas, *any* acompaña a sustantivos contables en plural y a sustantivos incontables. Se traduce por "ningún / ninguna" o "nada de".
We haven't got any potatoes. No tenemos patatas / ninguna patata.
There isn't any tea. No hay (nada de) té.

En las oraciones interrogativas, *any* acompaña a sustantivos contables en plural y a sustantivos incontables. Su traducción es "algunos / algunas" o "algo de".
Are there any chairs? ¿Hay alguna silla?
Is there any butter? ¿Hay (algo de) mantequilla?

! ¡Ojo!

En las oraciones interrogativas se utilizar *any*, pero cuando se ofrece o se pide algo también se puede utilizar *some*.

Do you want some strawberries? ¿Queréis unas fresas?
Would you like some coffee? ¿Le apetece un (poco de) café?
Can I have some popcorn, please? ¿Me pones unas palomitas, por favor?

much, many, a lot of

Countable and uncountable nouns

Los sustantivos contables tienen una forma para el singular y otra para el plural, y el verbo de la frase concuerda con ellos en número.
The pencil is in my bag. El lápiz está en mi bolsa.
The apples are in the fridge. Las manzanas están en la nevera.

Delante de los sustantivos contables se utilizan los artículos *a* / *an* y *the*, o bien un número.
an orange   the orange   two oranges

Los sustantivos incontables no tienen forma de plural. El verbo que los acompaña siempre va en singular.
cheese NO ~~two cheeses~~
The cheese is on the table. El queso está encima de la mesa.

Los sustantivos incontables no pueden ir precedidos del artículo *a* / *an*, ni tampoco de un número.
milk NO ~~one milk~~

There is ("hay") se utiliza con los sustantivos incontables.
There's some water in the bottle. Hay un poco de agua en la botella.

much, many, a lot of

Much significa "mucho / mucha". Se utiliza con sustantivos incontables en frases negativas o interrogativas.
'Is there much coffee?' 'Yes, but there isn't much milk.' "¿Hay mucho café?" "Sí, pero no hay mucha leche."

Many significa "muchos / muchas". Se utiliza con sustantivos contables en plural dentro de frases negativas o interrogativas.
'Are there many hamburgers?' 'No, and there aren't many sandwiches either.' "¿Hay muchas hamburguesas?" "No, y tampoco hay muchos sándwiches."

A lot of significa "mucho / mucha" y "muchos / muchas". Se utiliza con sustantivos contables e incontables en afirmativa.
There's a lot of washing. There are a lot of dirty glasses.
Hay mucha ropa para lavar. Hay muchos vasos sucios.

How much ...? / How many ...?

How much? significa "¿Cuánto / Cuánta?". Sólo se utiliza con los sustantivos incontables.
How much money have you got? ¿Cuánto dinero tienes?

How many? significa "¿Cuántos / Cuantas?". Sólo se utiliza con los sustantivos contables en plural.
How many books did she buy? ¿Cuántos libros compró?

have to

1 Complete the sentences. Use *have to* affirmative and negative.

My brother doesn't have to wear a uniform. ✗

1 You have to ______ be home early! ✓
2 Her parents don't have to work on Saturdays. ✗
3 Karen has to ______ share a bedroom with her sister. ✓
4 I don't have to study English at my school. ✗
5 We have to ______ walk to school every day. ✓
6 My history teacher has to ______ wear glasses. ✓

2 Write questions. Use *have to*. Then write true answers.

you / do the hoovering
Do you have to do the hoovering?
Yes, I do. / No, I don't.

1 your mum / do the washing every day?
Does your mum have to do the washing every day?
Students' answers
______
2 your friends / take the bus to school?
Do your friends have to take the bus to school?
______
______
3 your grandfather / wear glasses?
Does your grandfather have to wear glasses?
______
______
4 you / help with the housework at weekends?
Do you have to help with the housework at weekends?
______
5 you and your friends / study German at your school?
Do you and your friends have to study German at your school?
______

some and any

3 Complete the sentences. Use *some* or *any*.

We met some English students on holiday last year.

1 Is there any ______ salad in the fridge?
2 Have you got any ______ tickets for the match tomorrow?
3 Let's buy some ______ sweets before we see the film.
4 I didn't get any ______ emails yesterday.
5 Would you like some ______ ice cream?

much, many, a lot of

4 Are the nouns countable or uncountable? Write C or U.

	euro	C	4	bread	U
1	butter	U	5	money	U
2	biscuit	C	6	banana	C
3	juice	U	7	rice	U

5 Choose the correct options.

There isn't (**much**) / **many** water.

1 There aren't **much** / (**many**) flowers in our garden this year.
2 Are there **much** / (**a lot of**) teachers at your school?
3 There weren't **much** / (**many**) people at the concert last night.
4 I haven't got (**much**) / **many** homework today.
5 There's **much** / (**a lot of**) food. Let's make a nice lunch!

6 Complete the questions. Use *How much* and *How many*.

How much time have you got before lunch?

1 How many ______ hamburgers are there?
2 How much ______ salad is there in the fridge?
3 How many ______ people in your family have got dark eyes?
4 How many ______ exams have you got this month?
5 How much ______ rice do we need tonight?

Comparative and superlative adjectives

Spelling rules: comparative adjectives

1 Si el adjetivo tiene una sola sílaba (*short adjective*), se añade *-er*.
long / longer

2 Si acaba en una *-e* muda, se añade *-r*.
nice / nicer

3 Si acaba en una vocal y una consonante, la consonante final se duplica y se añade *-er*.
hot / hotter

4 Si acaba en consonante + *-y*, la *y* se transforma en *i* y se añade *-er*.
pretty / prettier

5 Si tiene dos o más sílabas (*long adjective*), se coloca *more* delante del adjetivo.
dangerous / more dangerous

Algunos adjetivos tienen formas irregulares en el grado comparativo.

Formas irregulares	
Adjetivo	**Comparativo**
good	better
bad	worse
far	further

Usos

Los adjetivos en grado comparativo se utilizan para comparar dos cosas o personas entre sí.

Valencia is big, but Madrid is bigger. Valencia es grande, pero Madrid es aún más grande.

! ¡Ojo!

Cuando se quieren comparar distintos grados de una cualidad, se utiliza *than* detrás del adjetivo en grado comparativo.

Ann is prettier than Beth. NO ~~Ann is prettier that Beth.~~ Ann es más guapa que Beth.

Spelling rules: superlative adjectives

1 Si el adjetivo tiene una sola sílaba (*short adjective*), se añade *-est*.
long / longest

2 Si acaba en una *-e* muda, se añade *-st*.
nice / nicest

3 Si acaba en una vocal y una consonante, la consonante final se duplica y se añade *-est*.
hot / hottest

4 Si acaba en consonante + *-y*, la *y* se transforma en *i* y se añade *-est*.
pretty / prettiest

5 Si tiene dos o más sílabas (*long adjective*), se coloca *most* delante del adjetivo.
dangerous / most dangerous

El superlativo exige colocar el artículo *the* delante del adjetivo.

nice / the nicest
hot / the hottest
important / the most important

Los adjetivos en grado superlativo se utilizan para comparar tres o más cosas o personas entre sí, cuando se quiere indicar que una es superior a las demás.

June 21st is the longest day of the year. El 21 de junio es el día más largo del año.
I think chemistry is the most difficult subject. Yo creo que la química es la asignatura más difícil.

Los adjetivos que tienen formas irregulares de comparativo también son irregulares en el superlativo.

Adjetivo	Comparativo	Superlativo
good	better	best
bad	worse	worst
far	further	furthest

En el superlativo se pueden construir preguntas con *What's? / Which is?* o *Who's?* ¿Cuál es? / ¿Quién es?
What's the most famous monument in France? ¿Cuál es el monumento más famoso de Francia?
Which is the biggest city in Europe? ¿Cuál es el país más grande de Europa?
Who's the best actress on TV? ¿Quién es la mejor actriz de la tele?

! ¡Ojo!

La preposición *in* se utiliza con el adjetivo en grado superlativo para destacar a un miembro del grupo.

China is the biggest country in the world.
NO ~~China is the biggest country of the world.~~
China es el país más grande del mundo.

too and *enough*

Too + adjetivo significa "demasiado".

She didn't speak to Daniel. She felt too nervous. No habló con Daniel. Estaba demasiado nerviosa.

Adjetivo + *enough* significa "lo bastante, lo suficientemente".

I can't reach that shelf. I'm not tall enough. No llego a esa estantería. No soy lo bastante alto.

Comparative and superlative adjectives

1 Write the comparative forms of the adjectives.

big bigger
1 far further
2 confident more confident
3 shy shyer
4 cheerful more cheerful
5 lazy lazier
6 beautiful more beautiful
7 bad worse
8 fast faster
9 brave braver

2 Complete the sentences. Use the comparative forms of the adjectives in the box.

cheap cold easy exciting ~~good~~

My football team's results were terrible last year. I hope they're better this year.
1 These trousers are too expensive. I want cheaper ones.
2 The weather was hot yesterday, but it's colder today.
3 *X-Men* is a bit boring, but *Wolverine* is more exciting .
4 German is difficult for a Spanish speaker. French is easier .

3 Complete the sentences. Use your opinions. Choose the adjective you believe is true and use the comparative and *than*.

I think …
… fresh fruit is healthier than ice cream. (healthy / unhealthy)
1 … girls are ______________ boys. (hard-working / lazy)
2 … a car is ______________ a motorbike. (comfortable / uncomfortable)
3 … football is ______________ basketball. (boring / interesting)
4 … cats are ______________ dogs. (friendly / unfriendly)

4 Write the superlative forms of the adjectives.

outgoing the most outgoing
1 big the biggest
2 quiet the quietest
3 healthy the healthiest
4 bad the worst
5 ambitious the most ambitious
6 nice the nicest
7 good the best
8 tidy the tidiest
9 far the furthest

5 Complete the sentences. Use superlatives.

In my opinion the Sagrada Familia is the most beautiful building in Spain. (beautiful)
1 I think the oldest woman alive is 122 years old. (old)
2 The fastest climb to the top of Everest took eight hours and ten minutes. (fast)
3 I think the Natural History Museum is the most interesting museum in London. (interesting)
4 The shortest person in the world is 74.1 centimetres tall. (short)

too and *enough*

6 Complete the sentences. Use the phrases in the box.

not big enough not confident enough not old enough too cold ~~too expensive~~ too untidy

This DVD costs 45 euros. It's too expensive!
1 I can't wear these shoes. They're not big enough .
2 I can't find anything in my wardrobe. It's too untidy .
3 Sam never speaks to girls. He's not confident enough .
4 You're not old enough to drive a car.
5 We can't go out tonight. It's too cold !

Present perfect affirmative and negative

Afirmativa	Formas contractas
I have finished	I've finished
you have finished	you've finished
he has finished	he's finished
she has finished	she's finished
it has finished	it's finished
we have finished	we've finished
you have finished	you've finished
they have finished	they've finished

Forma afirmativa: sujeto + *have / has* + participio pasado del verbo principal.

Toni has finished his book. Toni ha acabado su libro.

La forma del participio pasado de los verbos regulares es igual que la forma del *past simple*: el infinitivo del verbo + *-ed*.

work / worked   listen / listened

La forma del participio pasado de los verbos irregulares suele ser diferente a la forma del *past simple*. Los verbos irregulares no siguen reglas ortográficas establecidas. Tendrás que aprendértelos de memoria en el apartado de verbos irregulares que aparece al final del libro.

go / went / been / gone
see / saw / seen
drink / drank / drunk
have / had / had

La forma *been* se suele utilizar como participio pasado del verbo *go*.

We've been skateboarding. Hemos estado andando en monopatín.

Consulta la lista de verbos irregulares en el interior de la contraportada.

Negativa	Formas contractas
I have not finished	I haven't finished
you have not finished	you haven't finished
he has not finished	he hasn't finished
she has not finished	she hasn't finished
it has not finished	it hasn't finished
we have not finished	we haven't finished
you have not finished	you haven't finished
they have not finished	they haven't finished

Forma negativa: sujeto + negativa de *have / has* + participio pasado del verbo principal.

I haven't done my homework. No he hecho los deberes.

Spelling rules: past participle (regular verbs)

1 Con la mayoría de los verbos, se añade *-ed* al infinitivo del verbo sin *to*.
listen / listened   work / worked

2 Si el verbo acaba en una *-e* muda, se añade *-d*.
like / liked   arrive / arrived

3 Si acaba en consonante + *y*, la *y* se transforma en *i* y se añade *-ed*.
worry / worried   study / studied

4 Si el verbo acaba en una vocal y una consonante, la consonante final se duplica y se añade *-ed*.
stop / stopped   chat / chatted

5 Los verbos que terminan en *-y* no duplican la consonante final.
play / played

Usos

El *present perfect* se utiliza para hablar de un estado o de una acción que se inició en el pasado y continúa en este momento. También se utiliza para describir una experiencia del pasado.

I've lost my camera. He perdido la cámara de fotos. La perdí en el pasado y aún no la he encontrado.
She's always lived in Seville. Siempre ha vivido en Sevilla. Nació allí y sigue viviendo allí.
My sister has been snorkelling. Mi hermana ha practicado buceo con tubo.

El *present perfect* nunca se utiliza con expresiones de tiempo que se refieren a un momento concreto del pasado, aunque este sea muy reciente. Se utiliza cuando no importa o no sabemos exactamente cuándo ocurrió la acción.

We had dinner at nine o'clock. NO ~~We've had dinner at two o'clock.~~ Hemos cenado a las nueve.
We've had dinner. Ya hemos cenado. No importa la hora exacta.

Present perfect with *just*

El *present perfect* con *just* se utiliza para hablar de una acción que acaba de producirse.

Forma afirmativa: sujeto + *have / has* + *just* + participio pasado del verbo principal.

I've just sent him a text message. Acabo de mandarle un mensaje de texto.

Present perfect affirmative and negative

1 Write the past participles.

leave *left*

1 put *put*
2 do *done*
3 break *broken*
4 hear *heard*
5 try *tried*
6 win *won*
7 chat *chatted*
8 meet *met*
9 start *started*
10 play *played*
11 write *written*

2 Complete the sentences. Use the present perfect affirmative.

Hurray! We*'ve won* the prize. (win)

1 He's exhausted. He *'s run* all the way here. (run)
2 Great! I *'ve finished* all the ironing. (finish)
3 What's that song? It *'s been* on the radio three times today. (be)
4 My grandparents *have visited* Rome three times. (visit)

3 Write sentences. Use the present perfect negative.

We / not be / to the Vicente Calderón stadium.
We haven't been to the Vicente Calderón stadium.

1 John / not study / French.
John hasn't studied French.
2 My parents / not travel / by boat before.
My parents haven't travelled by boat before.
3 Susie / not tidy / her wardrobe.
Susie hasn't tidied her wardrobe.
4 I / not see / the Harry Potter films.
I haven't seen the Harry Potter films.
5 You / not try / windsurfing.
You haven't tried windsurfing.

4 Choose the correct options.

Good! He's **done** / **did** all the hoovering. (*done*)

1 They **haven't gone** / **didn't go** to school last week. (*didn't go*)
2 Our team **has played** / **played** a terrible match yesterday. (*played*)
3 Oh no! I**'ve lost** / **lost** my favourite sunglasses! (*'ve lost*)
4 She **hasn't been** / **didn't go** bungee jumping. She's too scared. (*hasn't been*)
5 We**'ve sent** / **sent** her three emails yesterday, but she hasn't replied. (*sent*)

Present perfect with *just*

5 Complete the sentences. Use the present perfect affirmative with *just*.

You can't go out now. It*'s just started* to snow. (start)

1 We're so sorry. We *'ve just heard* about your car accident. (hear)
2 I think our neighbours are very lucky. They *'ve just won* a car! (win)
3 'Where's Linda?' 'Oh, she *'s just left* to go to the gym.' (leave)
4 My grandfather's very sad. He *'s just lost* his dog. (lose)
5 Let's go for a ride. I *'ve just bought* a new bike! (buy)

Present perfect interrogative

Interrogativa	Respuestas breves	
	Afirmativa	Negativa
Have I finished?	Yes, I have.	No, I haven't.
Have you finished?	Yes, you have.	No, you haven't.
Has he finished?	Yes, he has.	No, he hasn't.
Has she finished?	Yes, she has.	No, she hasn't.
Has it finished?	Yes, it has.	No, it hasn't.
Have we finished?	Yes, we have.	No, we haven't.
Have you finished?	Yes, you have.	No, you haven't.
Have they finished?	Yes, they have.	No, they haven't.

Forma interrogativa: *Have / Has* + sujeto + participio pasado del verbo principal.

Have you met the new teacher? ¿Has tenido ocasión de conocer al nuevo profesor?

En las respuestas breves afirmativas no se utilizan las formas contractas; por el contrario, en las respuestas breves negativas es más frecuente utilizar las formas contractas.

'Have you sent an email to Peter?' 'Yes, I have.' NO ~~'Yes, I've.'~~ "¿Has enviado un email a Peter?" "Sí."

El *present perfect* se utiliza a menudo para preguntar por acciones y experiencias que se han realizado recientemente.

'Have you bought any new CDs recently?' 'Yes, I have. / No, I haven't.' "¿Has comprado algún CD nuevo últimamente?" "Sí. / No."

Consulta la lista de verbos irregulares en el interior de la contraportada.

How long ...?; *for* and *since*

Se utilizan *for* y *since* con el *present perfect* para hablar de la duración de una situación o acción que comenzó en el pasado y continúa en la actualidad.

Se utiliza *for* para referirse a la duración de la acción o la situación.

I've been at this school for three and a half years. Llevo tres años y medio en este instituto.
Tom has known Adela for seven months. Hace siete meses que Tom conoce a Adela.

Se utiliza *since* para referirse al momento en el que se inició la acción o la situación.

I've been at this school since 2005. Llevo en este instituto desde el año 2005.
Tom has known Adela since November. Tom conoce a Adela desde noviembre.

¡Ojo!

Cuando hablamos de una acción que se inició en el pasado y continúa en este momento, debemos utilizar el *present perfect*, nunca el *present simple*.

Tom has known Adela for seven months. NO ~~Tom knows Adela for seven months.~~ Hace siete meses que Tom conoce a Adela.)
I have studied English since 1996. NO ~~I study English since 1996.~~ Estudio inglés desde 1996.

How long ...? se utiliza con el *present perfect* para preguntar cuánto tiempo ha durado una situación o acción que comenzó en el pasado y continúa en este momento.

'How long have you lived here?' NO ~~'How long do you live here?'~~
'We've lived here for eight months / since July.' "¿Cuánto tiempo lleváis viviendo aquí?" "Vivimos aquí desde hace ocho meses / desde julio."

Present perfect interrogative

1 Rewrite the sentences to make questions.

She's been to London.
Has she been to London?

1 He's bought the newspaper.
Has he bought the paper?

2 They've left for school.
Have they left for school?

3 You've been shopping.
Have you been shopping?

4 They've finished their homework.
Have they finished their homework?

2 Write questions. Then write true answers.

you / ride a motorbike
Have you ridden a motorbike?
Yes, I have. / No, I haven't.

1 you / eat Chinese food
Have you eaten Chinese food?
Students' answers

2 you / try kite surfing
Have you tried kite surfing?

3 you / win a prize
Have you won a prize?

4 you / see a lion
Have you seen a lion?

3 Write sentences. Use the present perfect affirmative, negative and interrogative.

What / you do this morning?
What have you done this morning?

1 I / not see Oscar since last Sunday.
I haven't seen Oscar since last Sunday.

2 We / just come back from holiday.
We've just come back from holiday.

3 They / not eat chocolate for three days.
They haven't eaten chocolate for three days.

4 you / meet my brother, Sam?
Have you met my brother, Sam?

5 He / live in this house for a long time.
He's lived in this house for a long time.

How long ...?; *for* and *since*

4 Put the words in the box in the correct columns.

~~2004~~ a year December five o'clock four days last week seven months ten weeks two years Wednesday

for	since
a year	2004
four days	December
seven months	five o'clock
ten weeks	last week
two years	Wednesday

5 Complete the sentences. Use *for* and *since*.

We've been on holiday since last Friday.

1 My parents have been married for 30 years.

2 I've been at school today since 9 a.m.

3 Jane has worked there for eight weeks.

4 You've lived in Manchester for four months.

5 My friends have been away since 9th August.

6 Make questions. Use *How long*.

Lucy lives in Italy.
How long has Lucy lived in Italy?

1 Helen is in a band.
How long has Helen been in a band?

2 My brothers do karate.
How long have my brothers done karate?

3 My mum plays the piano.
How long has my mum played the piano?

4 I have a dog.
How long have I had a dog?

5 They know Rachel.
How long have they known Rachel?

will

Afirmativa	Forma contracta
I / you / he / she / it / we / you / they will go	I'll / you'll / he'll / she'll / it'll / we'll / you'll / they'll go

Forma afirmativa: sujeto + *will* + infinitivo del verbo sin *to*.

I'll phone you tonight. Te llamaré esta noche. / Esta noche te llamo.

Negativa	Forma contracta
I / you / he / she / it / we / you / they will not go	I / you / he / she / it / we / you / they won't go

Forma negativa: sujeto + *won't* + infinitivo del verbo sin *to*. En las frases negativas se suele utilizar la forma contracta.

She won't be at the party today – she's ill. Hoy no irá a la fiesta. Está enferma.

Interrogativa	Respuestas breves	
	Afirmativa	Negativa
Will I / you / he / she / it / we / you / they go?	Yes, I / you / he / she / it / we / you / they will.	No, I / you / he / she / it / we / you / they won't.

Forma interrogativa: *Will* + sujeto + infinitivo del verbo sin *to*.

Will you come before ten o'clock? ¿Vendrás antes de las diez?

En las respuestas breves negativas se suele utilizar la forma contracta.

'Will Susie help us?' 'Yes, she will.' / 'No, she won't.' "¿Nos ayudará Susie?" "Sí." / "No."

En las respuestas breves no se utiliza la contracción "sujeto + *'ll*".

Yes, he will. / No, he won't. NO ~~Yes, he'll. / No, he'll not.~~

Usos

Will y *won't* se utilizan para hablar del futuro en general, y también para hacer una predicción.

I'll text you tonight. Esta noche te mandaré/mando un mensaje.
Next year Cristiano Ronaldo will move to another team. Cristiano Ronaldo cambiará de equipo el año que viene.

Es frecuente que *will / won't* aparezcan detrás del verbo *think*.

I think I'll live in another country. Creo que viviré en otro país.
I don't think I'll pass my science exam. No creo que apruebe el examen de ciencias.

También se utiliza *will* para expresar decisiones que se toman mientras se habla.

'Who's next?' 'I'll have a go.' "¿Quién va ahora?" "Ya lo intento yo."

First conditional

Afirmativa	Forma contracta
If you win, we will go to the café.	If you win, we'll go to the café.

Forma afirmativa: *If* + sujeto + *present simple*, sujeto + *will* + infinitivo del verbo sin *to*.

Negativa	Forma contracta
If it rains, we will not go to the park.	If it rains, we won't go to the park.

Forma negativa: *If* + sujeto + *present simple*, sujeto + *won't* + infinitivo del verbo sin *to*.

Es más frecuente utilizar las formas contractas:

sujeto + *'ll* / sujeto + *won't*.

Cuando la proposición condicional encabeza la frase, va seguida de una coma. Sin embargo, la coma no es necesaria si la condicional aparece detrás de la proposición principal.

If you win, we'll go to the disco with you. / We'll go to the disco with you if you win. Si ganáis vosotros, os acompañaremos a la discoteca.

Usos

El condicional de primer grado o *first conditional* se utiliza para hablar de una situación que puede ocurrir, y es probable que ocurra, en el presente o en el futuro.

Las oraciones condicionales de primer grado constan de dos elementos:

La proposición condicional, encabezada por *If*, lleva el verbo en *present simple*, y expresa la condición necesaria para que una acción se cumpla.

La proposición principal, que incluye *will* + el infinitivo del verbo sin *to*, describe el resultado de la acción.

If you give me the pen, I'll show you how to do it. Si me das el bolígrafo, te enseñaré cómo hacerlo.

Para construir la forma negativa, se debe decidir cuál de los verbos de la frase tendrá que ir en negativa.

If he doesn't arrive soon, I'll miss the bus. Si no llega pronto, perderé el autobús.
If I watch the film at 10 p.m., I won't get up early tomorrow. Si veo la película de las 10 de la noche, no me levantaré temprano mañana.
If we don't study, we won't pass our exams. Si no estudiamos, no aprobaremos los exámenes.

will

1 Write affirmative and negative sentences. Use *will*.

Paul / not turn off the radio.
Paul won't turn off the radio.

1 I / phone him later.
I'll phone him later.

2 I / buy the cable for the computer.
I'll buy the cable for the computer.

3 We / not study for a long time.
We won't study for a long time.

4 He / text you tonight.
He'll text you tonight.

2 Write questions about Laura's future. Use *will*. Then write short answers.

live in France ✗
Will Laura live in France? No, she won't.

1 travel to England ✓
Will Laura travel to England? Yes, she will.

2 make new friends ✓
Will Laura make new friends? Yes, she will.

3 work with computers ✗
Will Laura work with computers? No, she won't.

4 have any pets ✗
Will Laura have any pets? No, she won't.

5 become a writer ✓
Will Laura become a writer? Yes, she will.

3 Complete sentences. Use *will*.

I / pass my maths exam
I think I'll pass my maths exam.

1 we / go shopping on Saturday
I don't think we'll go shopping on Saturday.

2 Jorge / work in a hospital
I think Jorge will work in a hospital.

3 it / snow tomorrow
I think it will snow tomorrow.

4 they / have children
I don't think they'll have children.

First conditional

4 Complete the sentences. Use the phrases in the box.

I'll use my dictionary ~~it'll break~~
they won't arrive on time we'll go camping
we'll go to the beach

If you drop that bottle, it'll break.

1 If I don't understand the text, I'll use my dictionary.

2 If we buy a tent, we'll go camping.

3 If the weather is good, we'll go to the beach.

4 If they don't hurry up, they won't arrive on time.

5 Complete the sentences. Use the present simple and *will*, affirmative or negative.

If he sends me an email, I'll reply immediately. (reply)

1 If you go waterskiing, you'll love it. (go)

2 If you don't ask her again, she won't do it. (not ask)

3 If we stay at home, we'll be bored. (be)

4 If he doesn't pass his exams, his parents will be upset. (not pass)

6 Complete the sentences. Use the verbs in the box, and use the present simple or *will*, affirmative or negative.

go leave ~~miss~~ not listen not make

If they don't arrive soon, they'll miss the train.

1 If you don't listen in class, you won't understand.

2 If he doesn't make his bed, his mum will be angry.

3 If the weather is good, I'll go cycling tomorrow.

4 If we leave now, we won't be late.

Present passive affirmative, negative and interrogative

Afirmativa	Formas contractas
I am invited	I'm invited
you are invited	you're invited
he is invited	he's invited
she is invited	she's invited
it is invited	it's invited
we are invited	we're invited
you are invited	you're invited
they are invited	they're invited

Forma afirmativa: sujeto + verbo *be* + participio pasado.

We're all invited to the party. Todos estamos invitados a la fiesta.
Ice cream is made with milk. El helado se hace con leche.

Consulta en la página 76 la forma y la ortografía del participio pasado de los verbos regulares.

Consulta la lista de verbos irregulares en el interior de la contraportada.

Negativa	Formas contractas
I am not invited	I'm not invited
you are not invited	you aren't invited
he is not invited	he isn't invited
she is not invited	she isn't invited
it is not invited	it isn't invited
we are not invited	we aren't invited
you are not invited	you aren't invited
they are not invited	they aren't invited

Forma negativa: sujeto + negativa del verbo *be* + participio pasado.

Oranges aren't grown in Russia. Las naranjas no se cultivan en Russia.

Interrogativa	Respuestas breves	
	Afirmativa	Negativa
Am I invited?	Yes, I am.	No, I'm not.
Are you invited?	Yes, you are.	No, you aren't.
Is he invited?	Yes, he is.	No, he isn't.
Is she invited?	Yes, she is.	No, she isn't.
Is it invited?	Yes, it is.	No, it isn't.
Are we invited?	Yes, we are.	No, we aren't.
Are you invited?	Yes, you are.	No, you aren't.
Are they invited?	Yes, they are.	No, they aren't.

Forma interrogativa: *Am / Are / Is* + sujeto + participio pasado.

Are the eggs fried? ¿Se fríen los huevos?

En las respuestas breves negativas se suelen utilizar las formas contractas.

'Is tea grown in Ireland?' 'No, it isn't.' "¿El té se cultiva en Irlanda?" "No."

El objeto de una oración activa se corresponde con el sujeto de una oración pasiva.

They make Rolls Royce cars in Britain.
Rolls Royce cars are made in Britain.
Los coches Rolls Royce se hacen en Gran Bretaña.

! ¡Ojo!

La forma del participio pasado no varía nunca.

Of course he's invited to the disco. We're all invited.
NO ~~We're all inviteds.~~ Por supuesto que él está invitado a la discoteca. Todos estamos invitados.

Usos

La voz pasiva se utiliza cuando no se sabe o no importa quién realiza la acción.

Tea is imported from India. El té se importa de la India.
Waiters are paid £25. Los camareros cobran 25 libras.

Present passive affirmative, negative and interrogative

1 Write the past participles.

	find	found	6	serve	served
1	permit	permitted	7	make	made
2	eat	eaten	8	teach	taught
3	build	built	9	send	sent
4	drink	drunk	10	try	tried
5	grow	grown	11	speak	spoken

2 Rewrite the sentences to make them passive.

They send thousands of emails every minute.
Thousands of emails are sent every minute.

1 They eat sushi in Japan.
Sushi is eaten in Japan.

2 They make SEAT cars in Spain.
SEAT cars are made in Spain.

3 They grow excellent coffee in Colombia.
Excellent coffee is grown in Colombia.

4 They use mobile phones all the time.
Mobile phones are used all the time.

5 They teach French and English at our school.
French and English are taught at our school.

3 Complete the sentences. Use the present passive affirmative and negative of the verbs in the box.

clean not eat ~~not permit~~
not sell pay serve

Mobile phones are not permitted in class.

1 In Britain, fish is served with chips.

2 My friend works in a café. She is paid eight euros per hour.

3 Meat is not eaten by vegetarians.

4 The classrooms in our school are cleaned every evening.

5 In Spain cigarettes are not sold to children – it's illegal.

4 Write questions. Use the present passive.

When / New Year / celebrate in Britain?
When is New Year celebrated in Britain?

1 Where / paella / eat?
Where is paella eaten?

2 When / rice / throw at people?
When is rice thrown at people?

3 Where / coffee / grow?
Where is coffee grown?

4 How often / the Olympic Games / hold?
How often are the Olympic Games held?

5 Answer the questions in exercise 4. Use the phrases in the box.

at weddings every four years in Colombia
in Valencia ~~on 1 January~~

New Year is celebrated in Britain on 1 January.

1 Paella is eaten in Valencia.

2 Rice is thrown at people at weddings.

3 Coffee is grown in Colombia.

4 The Olympic Games are held every four years.

6 Complete the paragraph. Use the present passive affirmative, negative and interrogative.

Many food products – for example, tea, coffee, rice, bananas and melons – are imported (import) into Britain from poorer countries. A lot of the workers in poorer countries (1) are not paid (not pay) much money. An organization called Fairtrade wants to change this. Fairtrade products (2) are grown (grow) in poorer countries and they (3) are brought (bring) to Britain by boat or plane. The products (4) are sent (send) to certain supermarkets and shops. After the products (5) are sold (sell), the profits (6) are shared (share) equally between the supermarkets and the workers. Sometimes the workers (7) are not given (not give) money. They (8) are sent (send) seeds to grow new crops or food for their own families. A lot of people (9) are helped (help) by Fairtrade. (10) Are Fairtrade products sold (sell) in your country?

Words to learn

Leisure activities

chess ______
computer games ______
cooking ______
cycling ______
dancing ______
drawing ______
fashion ______
films ______
keeping fit ______
magazines ______
music ______
photography ______
sport ______
the Internet ______

Noun endings

activity ______
argument ______
collection ______
entertainment ______
location ______
possibility ______
quality ______
reaction ______
situation ______
treatment ______

Verb + noun collocation

take photos ______
send texts ______
meet friends ______
do aerobics ______
visit chat rooms ______
have a meal out ______
play basketball ______
go jogging ______

Phrases to learn

I'm a big fan of … ______
I'm mad about … ______
I'm quite interested in … ______
I'm (not) really into … ______
I'm very keen on … ______

Leisure activities

1 yoga ______________________________

2 horse riding ______________________________

3 juggling ______________________________

4 drama ______________________________

5 singing ______________________________

6 pottery ______________________________

7 knitting ______________________________

8 hiking ______________________________

Words to learn

Describing feelings

confused ______
cross ______
delighted ______
embarrassed ______
exhausted ______
relaxed ______
scared ______
surprised ______
upset ______
disappointed ______
excited ______
fed up ______
irritated ______
jealous ______
lonely ______
nervous ______

Verbs of movement

dive ______
climb ______
crawl ______
fall ______
jump ______
run ______
walk ______
wander ______

Prepositions of movement

along ______
away from ______
into ______
off ______
onto ______
out of ______
past ______
round ______
towards ______

Phrases to learn

Did you have a good weekend? ______
______
What did you do? ______
It was(n't) great. ______

Describing feelings

1 miserable ______________________

4 amazed ______________________

2 shocked ______________________

5 stressed ______________________

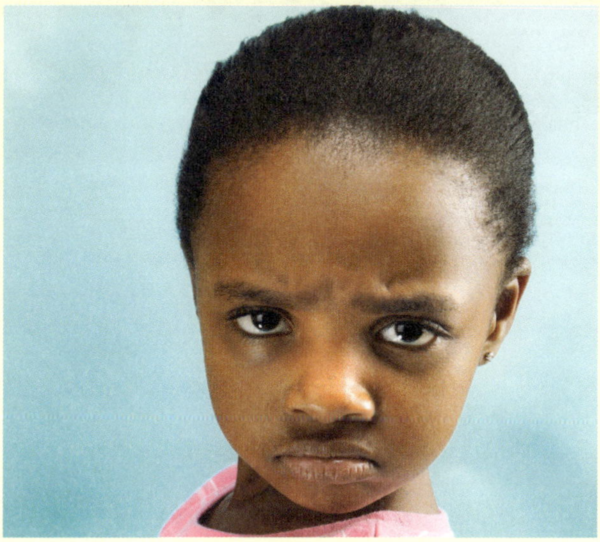

3 annoyed ______________________

6 worried ______________________

Words to learn

Crime

arson ______
burglary ______
drug dealing ______
hacking ______
joyriding ______
murder ______
shoplifting ______
theft ______
vandalism ______
speeding ______

Adjective endings

rainy ______
beautiful ______
optional ______
famous ______
dangerous ______
cloudy ______
powerful ______
national ______
mysterious ______
healthy ______
careful ______
musical ______
colourful ______
dirty ______
juicy ______
natural ______
tasty ______

Phrases to learn

How about (read)ing? ______
What about (read)ing? ______
Why don't you / we (read)? ______

Crime

1 judge ____________________

2 handcuffs ____________________

3 prison ____________________

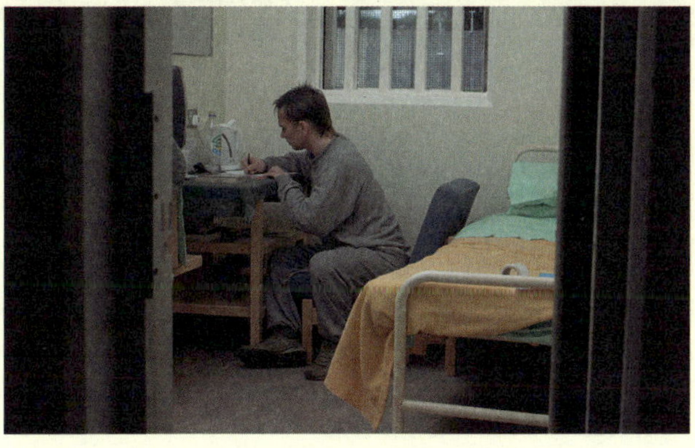

4 cell ____________________

5 court ____________________

6 jury ____________________

7 prisoner ____________________

8 witness ____________________

Words to learn

Household tasks

cooker ____________________

dustbin ____________________

ironing board ____________________

vacuum cleaner ____________________

washing machine ____________________

do the hoovering ____________________

do the cooking ____________________

make your bed ____________________

put the rubbish out ____________________

tidy up ____________________

do the washing ____________________

clean the floor ____________________

do the ironing ____________________

wash up ____________________

do the dusting ____________________

do the shopping ____________________

do the gardening ____________________

do, have, make

have a bath ____________________

make a cup of coffee ____________________

make dinner ____________________

have a drink ____________________

do the gardening ____________________

do homework ____________________

do the housework ____________________

make a phone call ____________________

have a rest ____________________

have an argument ____________________

make friends ____________________

have a good / terrible time ____________________

make a mistake ____________________

do somebody a favour ____________________

do some work ____________________

Phrases to learn

Would you like to (come to my party)? ____________________

Would you like (a drink)? ____________________

Yes, I'd love to. ____________________

I'm afraid I can't. ____________________

Sorry, but I won't be able to make it. ____________________

Yes, that sounds great. ____________________

In the garden

1 lawn ______________________________

2 hedge ______________________________

3 flower bed ______________________________

4 pond ______________________________

5 fence ______________________________

6 tools ______________________________

7 lawnmower ______________________________

8 hose ______________________________

Words to learn

Describing personality

ambitious ______
bad-tempered ______
big-headed ______
brave ______
cheerful ______
hard-working ______
selfish ______
shy ______
talkative ______
modest ______
outgoing ______
lazy ______
quiet ______
miserable ______

Compound adjectives

long-legged ______
dark-skinned ______
broad-shouldered ______
thin-lipped ______
kind-hearted ______
quick-witted ______
loud-mouthed ______
blue-eyed ______
high-ceilinged ______
fair-haired ______
long-sleeved ______
high-heeled ______
high-backed ______
thin-lipped ______
long-haired ______
green-skinned ______

Phrases to learn

not at all (bad-tempered) ______
not very (bad-tempered) ______
quite (bad-tempered) ______
very (bad-tempered) ______

Describing people

1 clumsy ______________________

2 graceful ______________________

3 dishonest ______________________

4 intelligent ______________________

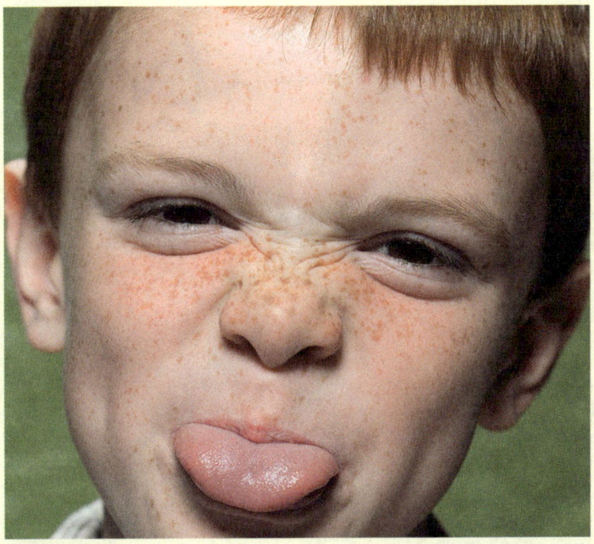

5 rude ______________________

6 adventurous ______________________

Words to learn

Adventure sports

BASE jumping ______
bungee jumping ______
caving ______
free running ______
hang-gliding ______
kayaking ______
kite surfing ______
rock climbing ______
skydiving ______
snorkelling ______
waterskiing ______
windsurfing ______

Adjective opposites

light ______
dark ______
heavy ______
quiet ______
loud ______
blunt ______
sharp ______
dirty ______
clean ______
dry ______
wet ______
high ______
low ______
rough ______
smooth ______
shallow ______
deep ______
soft ______
hard ______
strong ______
weak ______
wide ______
narrow ______

Phrases to learn

I've just (had lunch). ______
be broke ______
Have you ever (been windsurfing)? ______

First aid

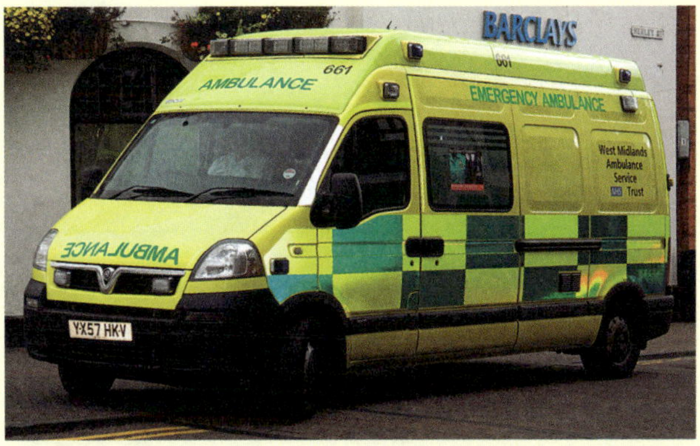

1 ambulance ______________________________

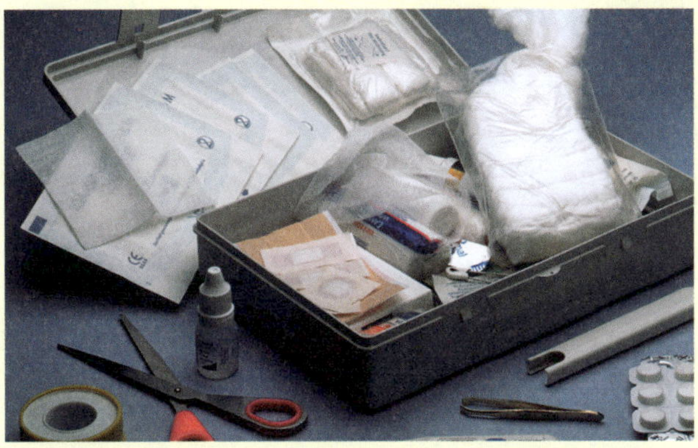

2 first-aid kit ______________________________

3 stretcher ______________________________

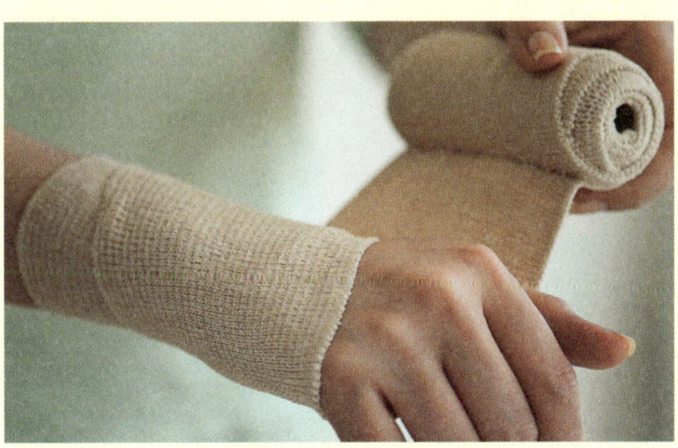

4 bandage ______________________________

5 broken arm ______________________________

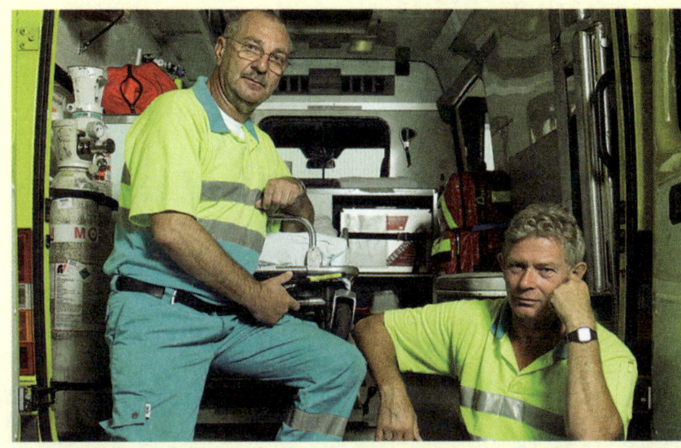

6 paramedics ______________________________

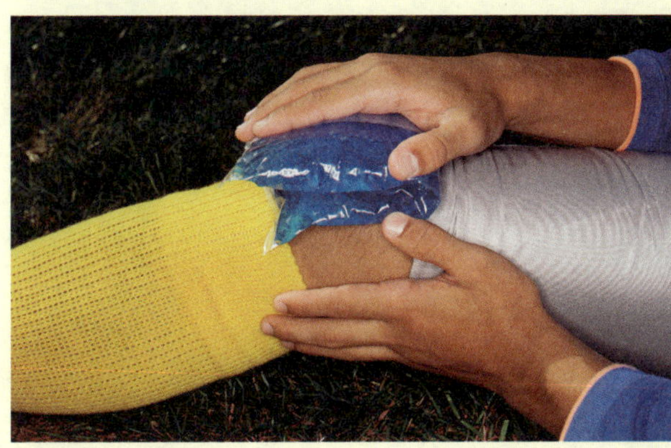

7 compress ______________________________

8 plaster ______________________________

Words to learn

In the high street

baker's ______
bank ______
bookshop ______
butcher's ______
chemist's ______
clothes shop ______
electrical store ______
estate agent's ______
florist's ______
hairdresser's ______
newsagent's ______
post office ______
takeaway ______
travel agent's ______

Synonyms and antonyms

begin / start ______
blunt / sharp ______
difficult / hard / easy ______
dry / wet ______
frightened / scared ______
shop / store ______
difficulties / problems ______
extremely / incredibly ______
correct / right ______
attractive / beautiful / ugly ______
quick / fast / slow ______
loud / noisy / quiet ______

False friends

sensible ______
fabric ______
exit ______
carpet ______
blank ______
absolutely ______
parents ______

Phrases to learn

How long (have you been a student)? ______
I'm going to (travel around the world). ______
Are you going to (travel to England)? ______

At the shops

1 counter ______________________

2 basket ______________________

3 trolley ______________________

4 receipt ______________________

5 carrier bag ______________________

6 cashier ______________________

7 check-out ______________________

8 discount ______________________

Words to learn

High-tech gadgets		Phrasal verbs	
Blu-ray player	______	turn on	______
camcorder	______	turn off	______
digital photo frame	______	pick up	______
games console	______	put down	______
sat nav	______	take off	______
wireless headset	______	put on	______
DAB radio	______	give in	______
MP3 player	______	give out	______
SCART cable	______	give away	______
USB hub	______	give back	______
		give up	______
		give (something) up	______

Phrases to learn

I think (Eric) will (go to the cinema).

______

I don't think (Sophie) will (go to the cinema).

______

I think you should (tell her). ______

I don't think you should (tell her). ______

You must (tell her). ______

On the one hand, ... ______

Furthermore, ... ______

On the other hand, ... ______

What is more, ... ______

I believe ... ______

In my opinion, ... ______

Technology

1 mobile phone recharger ______________________
____

2 projector ______________________

3 portable hard drive ______________________
____

4 memory stick ______________________

5 remote control ______________________

6 disc drive ______________________

7 hard drive ______________________

Words to learn

Food

beef ____________________
carrots ____________________
cheese ____________________
chicken ____________________
green beans ____________________
ham ____________________
mushrooms ____________________
olives ____________________
peas ____________________
peppers ____________________
potatoes ____________________
prawns ____________________
rice ____________________
tomato ____________________
cous cous ____________________
curry ____________________
fish and chips ____________________
haggis ____________________
moussaka ____________________
pasta ____________________
sushi ____________________
tortillas ____________________
protein ____________________
carbohydrates ____________________
fat ____________________

Partitives

a packet of biscuits ____________________
a bottle of wine ____________________
a carton of orange juice ____________________
a box of matches ____________________
a jar of jam ____________________
a bag of sweets ____________________
a tube of toothpaste ____________________
a can of cola ____________________
a carton of milk ____________________
a tube of glue ____________________
a bottle of water ____________________
a bag of shopping ____________________
a jar of green olives ____________________
a packet of chewing gum ____________________
a box of chocolates ____________________
a can of lemonade ____________________
a can / tube of paint ____________________
a bottle / carton / can of tomato juice ____________________
a packet / bag / box of pasta ____________________
a bag / box of oranges ____________________
a slice of bread / cheese ____________________
a piece of cake / chewing gum ____________________
a cup of coffee / tea ____________________
a spoonful of sugar / honey ____________________
a piece of chocolate ____________________
a spoonful of jam ____________________
a slice of meat ____________________

Phrases to learn

I'd like (a can of cola), please. ____________________
Could I have (a can of cola), please? ____________________

At the shops

1 raw (fish) ______________________

5 unripe (banana) ______________________

2 cooked (fish) ______________________

6 ripe (banana) ______________________

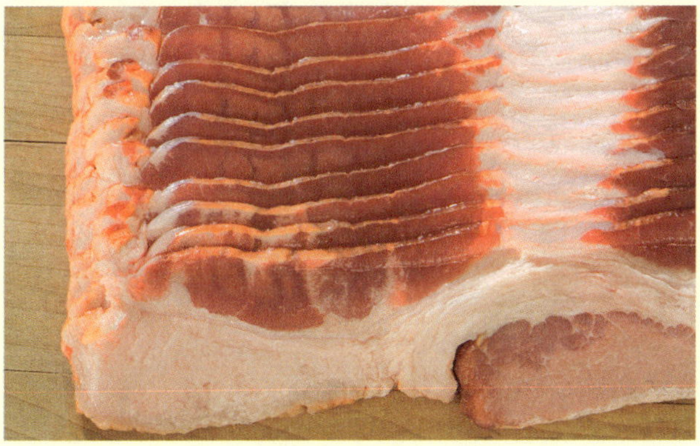

3 fatty (meat) ______________________

7 fresh (peas) ______________________

4 lean (meat) ______________________

8 frozen (peas) ______________________

Personal profile

1 Read the text.

We use different paragraphs for different topics.

Topic: home and family

Topic: school and ambitions

Topic: hobbies and interests

My friend Laura

My best friend's name is Laura. She's fifteen years old and she lives with her dad and her brother Josh. They've got two dogs, called Red and Blue.

Laura's in my class at St Thomas School for girls. She's in Year 10 and her favourite subjects are chemistry, history and biology. She's not very keen on French, German or art. At university, she wants to study medicine. She wants to become a doctor.

In her free time, Laura is really into music. She plays the saxophone, and she's in a band. They're really cool. Her other hobby is ice hockey, and she plays in an ice hockey team. We sometimes go ice skating at weekends, but I don't think Laura is a big fan.

Writing help Paragraphs

We use paragraphs for different topics. When you write, make notes to plan your topics and paragraphs. For example:

1	Home / family	15 Dad, Josh, dogs
2	School / ambitions	St Thomas, Year 10 Best / worst subjects University, work plans
3	Hobbies / interests	Music Ice hockey (ice skating)

2 Read the information. Match the sentences and the paragraph topics.

Paragraph topics

A Home and family
B School and ambitions
C Hobbies and interests

David's in Year 10 at Wood Green School. B

1 He lives in Croydon with his parents. A
2 He wants to study architecture at university. B
3 He's a big fan of computer games. C
4 He loves maths and science, but he doesn't like history or geography. B
5 David's really keen on swimming. He's in our school swimming team. C
6 He's fourteen years old. A

3 In your notebook, write a profile of your best friend. Make notes and use the writing guide.

Paragraph 1
Home and family
Paragraph 2
School and ambitions
Paragraph 3
Hobbies and interests

Account of events

1 Read the text.

We use sequencing words to order events in a story or an account of events.

My birthday

I had an interesting day last Saturday. This is what happened.

It was my fifteenth birthday, but it wasn't a good day. First of all, my mum was at work, and my dad was irritated. Then I had an argument with my sister.

Next, I phoned my best friend, Mike. 'Oh no!' he said. 'I forgot your birthday! I'm sorry.' I was cross, but Mike said, 'Let's go out.' An hour after that, I met Mike at our favourite café. But something was different – the café was dark.

When we walked in, the lights came on. All of my friends and family were in the café. 'Surprise!' they shouted. We had a wonderful party. There was music and we danced, and there was great food. Finally, everything went right. It was my best birthday ever.

Writing help **Sequencing words**

Remember that sequencing words help people to understand what they read. Help people understand you: use sequencing words when you write.

2 Choose the correct options.

Before / **First of all**, I felt excited when I woke up.

1 Ten minutes **later** / **after** breakfast, I had an argument with my sister.
2 I checked my email and **then** / **after** I looked at my phone, but there were no birthday emails or texts.
3 I talked to Mike on the phone, and **later** / **after** we met at the café.
4 **Before** / **Then** we arrived at the café, I felt really upset.
5 Everyone shouted 'Surprise!' **then** / **when** we arrived.
6 **When** / **Next** I saw my friends, I knew it was a surprise party.
7 **Before** / **When** the party, I felt cross with my friends.

3 In your notebook, write an account of events in an interesting day that you had. Make notes and use the writing guide.

Paragraph 1
I had an interesting day ....
This is what happened.

Paragraph 2
It was ....
First of all, ...
Then ....

Paragraph 3
Next, ...
After that ....

Paragraph 4
When ....
Finally, ...
It was ....

Describing a scene

1 Read the text.

When we use two continuous verbs together, we don't have to write the subject and *be* twice. We sometimes have to change *and* to *or* if the verbs are negative.

More concise than: **lots of people were walking and lots of people were chatting** on the street.

More concise than: **They were standing ... and they were looking** at the street.

The scene of the crime

When Detective Sharp arrived in Corn Street, he knew that something was wrong. It was a warm Saturday night, and the bars and restaurants were closing. Usually, at this time on a Saturday, lots of people were walking and chatting on the street. But tonight it wasn't busy. People weren't coming out of the bars and restaurants or going home. They were standing at the doors and windows, and looking at the street.

On one side of the street Detective Sharp saw three shops with broken windows. He also saw two other police officers and a young man in handcuffs. The young man had long hair. He was wearing dirty jeans and an old T-shirt. The police officers were asking him questions and he was looking guilty and frightened. But he wasn't saying anything.

There was also an elegant woman. She was wearing formal office clothes, and talking on a mobile phone. She wasn't running or looking guilty. But she was walking away from the crime scene – and carrying a big bag. Why was she wearing office clothes on a Saturday night? And what was in her bag?

More concise than: **People weren't coming out ... and people weren't going home.** Change *and* to *or*.

Two different subjects: **The police officers were asking** him questions **and looking** guilty and frightened. ✗

2 Rewrite the sentences more concisely. You may have to change *and* to *or*.

The burglar was picking up my laptop and he was putting it into his bag.
The burglar was picking up my laptop and putting it into his bag.

1 The gang weren't vandalizing the telephone box and they weren't breaking the law.
The gang weren't vandalizing the telephone box or breaking the law.

2 We weren't moving and we weren't speaking as the bank robbery took place.
We weren't moving or speaking as the bank robbery took place.

3 Many people were phoning the police and they were reporting the crime.
Many people were phoning the police and reporting the crime.

3 In your notebook, write a description of a crime scene. Make notes and use the writing guide. Remember to write concisely.

Paragraph 1
Who was the detective? Where was the scene of the crime? What was the weather like? What was happening?

Paragraph 2
Did the detective see any interesting people? Describe them. What were they doing?

Paragraph 3
Did the detective see anything else? Describe what he saw. Why was it interesting?

Article

1 Read the text.

We list adjectives in this order: opinion, size, age, shape, colour, origin, material + noun.

age

colour

origin

My favourite room

My favourite room is in my grandparents' house, near Calella, in Spain. The house is a traditional, old, stone house by the sea. The best room in the house is the living room. It's a big, long room, with white walls and a dark, wooden floor.

My grandparents' living room has got lots of lovely, large, old furniture. There's a long, white, English sofa with about ten green and pink cushions on it. There's also a big, square, wooden dining table. We have family dinners there when we visit my grandparents.

My favourite thing about the room is the windows. There are big windows with comfortable chairs under them. I love to sit there and look at the beautiful, blue sea and sky.

opinion

material

size

shape

Writing help Order of adjectives

If there are more than two adjectives before the noun, we usually separate them with commas.
There was a square, wooden table. ✓
There was a square and wooden table. ✗

If there is more than one colour before the noun, we separate the colours with *and*.
pink and green cushions ✓
pink, green cushions ✗

2 Complete the sentences. Use the words in the box.

and beautiful ~~glass~~ old
purple round small

I saw an Italian, glass bowl at the shop.

1 My mother has a large, old______, round mirror in her bedroom.
2 I want that long, purple______, French sofa.
3 Frances has a beautiful______, large, garden.
4 My aunt has some lovely, small______, old dining chairs.
5 My room has blue and______ white curtains.
6 There's a new, round______, black coffee table in our living room.

3 In your notebook, write an article about your favourite room. Make notes and use the writing guide.

Paragraph 1
Where is the house? Describe the house.
Is the room a kitchen / bedroom / living room ...?
Size? Walls? Floor? Windows?

Paragraph 2
Furniture? (List adjectives to describe the furniture.)

Paragraph 3
What is your favourite thing about the room?

Describing a fictional character

1 Read the text.

We often omit the subject pronoun after the conjunctions *and* and *but*. We don't omit the subject pronoun after most other conjunctions.

Omit the pronoun after *and* and *but*.

Don't omit the pronoun after other conjunctions.

Homer Simpson

Homer Simpson is a cartoon character in a TV series called *The Simpsons*. *The Simpsons* is one of the most successful cartoons in the world. The show is about Homer's family. Homer has a wife, Marge, and has three children, Bart, Lisa and Maggie. Homer works in a factory, but is terrible at his job. He never works unless he has no choice. He prefers to drink beer and watch TV.

Homer is big-eyed and yellow-skinned (like his family), and about 40 years old. He's quite fat, and hasn't got much hair. He wears casual clothes: a white shirt and blue jeans. Homer's wife loves him even though he's not a very attractive man.

Homer Simpson is an unusual hero, because he's lazy, greedy and ignorant. However, many people love him, even though he is terrible at everything. He's a kind-hearted man, and a very funny character.

2 Choose the best options.

Ugly Betty lives in New York, and **she works / works** for a fashion magazine, *Mode*.

1. Betty wears terrible clothes, even though **she works / works** at the *Mode* magazine offices.
2. Betty's boss, Daniel, doesn't work unless **he thinks / thinks** his secretary is unattractive.
3. Betty gets a job as Daniel's secretary because **she is / is** 'ugly'.
4. In the show, Betty works hard but **she never gets / never gets** respect at work.
5. The show started in Colombia, and **it exists / exists** in many different languages and countries.
6. The American show is more popular in many places, even though **it is / is** in English.

3 In your notebook, write a description of your favourite fictional character from a film or TV show. Make notes and use the writing guide. Remember to omit subject pronouns where you can.

Paragraph 1
What's the character's name? What's the name of the film or TV show? What is it about?

Paragraph 2
Describe the character's appearance and clothes.

Paragraph 3
Describe the character's personality. Why is it interesting? Why do people like this character?

Postcard

1 Read the text.

We can use informal language in postcards, informal letters and emails.

informal words

informal phrases

Hi Mike!

This is the third day of my holiday in London. The weather's been nice and sunny, and we've been busy every day. I've been shopping in loads of markets, and I bought some really fab clothes. I also met an old mate of mine, Sophie, and her boyfriend, a guy called Darren. Tomorrow, I want to go to some museums – most of the museums in London are free, and I'm broke!

Love

Katie

Writing help — Informal words and phrases

Don't forget the informal words you already know:
cool hi OK TV yeah

2 Rewrite the <u>underlined</u> words. Use informal language.

I've been to all the markets and now <u>I've got no money</u>. I'm broke

1. I want to try hang-gliding, but it costs <u>a lot of</u> money. loads of
2. I met a really cool <u>boy</u> when I went rock climbing. guy
3. Bungee jumping is <u>quite</u> exciting, but I like skydiving best! pretty
4. I've been bungee jumping once, and I hated it – it's really <u>frightening</u>! scary
5. I've only been waterskiing once, but it was absolutely <u>fabulous</u>. fab
6. I had a party with all my <u>friends</u>. mates
7. There was a programme about caving on the <u>television</u> last night. telly

3 In your notebook, write a postcard to your friend. Make notes and use the writing guide. Remember to use informal words and phrases.

Greet your friend.

- Say which day of your holiday it is.
- Say where you are.
- Say what the weather has been like.
- Tell your friend about two activities you have done on your holiday.
- Say what you want to do on the rest of your holiday.

End the postcard informally.

Informal letter

1 Read the text.

We often use subject pronouns, object pronouns and possessive adjectives to avoid repeating nouns.

subject pronoun

object pronoun

possessive adjective

Dear Aunt Amanda

I hope you're well! I'm sorry I haven't written to you for a long time. I've had a really busy year. (a) It's been hard work, but fun, and now I've finished almost all my exams. (b) They were difficult, but I studied hard and I think I've done okay.

After my last exam, I'm going to go to a music festival with all my friends. (c) We're going to have a brilliant time (d) there! Then I'm going to wait for my exam results – and I'm going to relax and have fun after my hard work!

Have you heard what's happened to Andy? (e) He fell off (f) his bike and (g) he's broken (h) his leg! (i) It's painful, but the doctors say (j) it'll be fine. (k) He says (l) he's very bored with (m) it, and (n) he's going to do a bike race when (o) it's better.

Lots of love

Jock

2 Read the letter in exercise 1 again. Match pronouns (a) to (o) with the things below.

1 Andy's leg (i) (j) (m) (o)
2 my exams (b)
3 my year (a)
4 Andy (e) (g) (k) (l) (n)
5 my friends and I (c)
6 at the music festival (d)
7 Andy's (f) (h)

3 Rewrite the underlined words. Avoid repeating nouns. Use the words in the box.

he	our	~~that~~	there	they	us

'Do you want to see a film tonight?' 'Yes, I'd love ~~to see a film~~. that

1 I spent the afternoon with Jamie. ~~Jamie~~'s split up with his girlfriend. He
2 We went to Corsica for our holiday. We had a great time ~~in Corsica~~. there
3 My cousin came to stay with my family, and he broke ~~my family's and my~~ TV! our
4 I saw Alicia and her boyfriend last night. ~~Alicia and her boyfriend~~ are having a lot of arguments. They
5 Dan met ~~my friends and I~~ at the beach. us

4 In your notebook, write an informal letter to someone in your family. Make notes and use the writing guide. Remember to avoid repeating nouns.

Dear …

Paragraph 1
Your news and recent events

Paragraph 2
Your plans for the near future

Paragraph 3
Information about a friend or someone in your family

Essay: for and against

1 Read the text.

In an essay where we look at arguments for and against something, we present one side of the argument, then present the other side of the argument, and finally express our own opinions.

present one side

present the other side

express your own opinion

Life will be easier in the future

Will life be easier in the future? There are arguments for this and against it.

On the one hand, technology is making our lives easier all the time. Modern life is much safer, cleaner and quicker than life was for our parents and grandparents. We can travel and study more easily, and we have more options than in the past. Furthermore, we live much longer, because doctors, hospitals and medicine are better.

On the other hand, if we live longer, people will work until they are 70 or 80, or even older. What is more, environmental problems like climate change will get worse in the future. This will affect air travel, energy problems and pollution. It won't be possible to do some things that are easy now.

I believe that life will be easier in some ways, and harder in other ways. In my opinion, home life will become better, with lots of new technology. But our environmental problems will be a lot worse, and I think this will be more important.

2 Correct the underlined phrases.

Jobs are more stressful than in the past. That is more, people are working more.
What is more

1 On the one side, technology will help us to find alternative fuels.
On the one hand

2 On other hand, communication will continue to get faster and easier.
On the other hand

3 By my opinion, the Internet is bad for children's social skills.
In my opinion

4 Further, we may have more economic problems in the future.
Furthermore

5 I am believe that we will need new laws restricting energy use.
I believe

3 In your notebook, write an essay about the statement below. Make notes and use the writing guide.

'The environment will be the only important issue in the 21st century.'

Paragraph 1: introduction
Will the environment be ...?
There are arguments ...

Paragraph 2: present one side
On the one hand ...
Furthermore ...

Paragraph 3: present the other side
On the other hand ...
What is more ...

Paragraph 4: express your own opinion
I believe ...
In my opinion ...

Describing your worst meal

1 Read the text.

When you write, check your spelling, punctuation and grammar.

Check grammar (for example: the superlative form)

Check spelling (for example: words that are similar in your language)

Check punctuation (for example: no exclamation mark at the start of a sentence)

A terrible meal

The worst meal I've ever had was the first time I had dinner with my girlfriend, Maria. It was a Saturday evening last year, and we went to a new Mexican restaurant, because Maria likes Mexican tortillas.

The weather was terrible that night, and it was raining as we walked to the restaurant, so we got cold and wet. At the restaurant, they gave us a table next to the door, and every time somebody went in or out it was very cold. We were both a bit annoyed, but it was worse when the food arrived – an hour later!

I had tortillas with chicken and Spanish rice, but there was so much chilli in the chicken that I couldn't eat it. Maria ordered black bean tortillas, but they gave her beef tortillas. Maria doesn't eat meat! We had a terrible night, and a terrible meal.

Writing help **Checking your work**

When you check your grammar, remember to check that you have chosen the correct tense and remember which verbs are irregular.

2 Read the description of a meal. Correct the mistakes.

My first dinner with my boyfriend was a ~~meal strange~~. We ~~were~~ to a ~~beatiful~~ French restaurant outside our town. It was a very elegant restaurant, ~~and was~~ classical music playing. The waiters were very polite. It was fabulous. Then our food came. My boyfriend ~~eat~~ chicken and ~~i~~ had beef. ~~¡It~~ looked great, but it was cold! After the meal, we ~~have~~ a lovely walk on the beach. It ~~has been~~ a very strange occasion. The restaurant was ~~fabulos~~ and the walk on the beach was lovely, but the food was terrible.

strange meal
1 went
2 beautiful
3 and there was
4 ate
5 I
6 It
7 had
8 was
9 fabulous

3 In your notebook, write a description of your worst meal. Make notes and use the writing guide. Remember to check your spelling, punctuation and grammar.

Paragraph 1
What was the occasion?
Who was there?
When did you have the meal?
Where did you eat?

Paragraph 2
What happened before you ate?
Before the food, was the occasion good or bad?

Paragraph 3
What did you eat?
Why was the food bad?
Your overall opinion of the meal and the occasion.

Vowels		Consonants	
/i/	happy	/p/	pen
/ɪ/	it	/b/	big
/iː/	he	/t/	two
/æ/	cat	/d/	dog
/ɑː/	art	/k/	can
/e/	egg	/g/	good
/ɜː/	girl	/tʃ/	cheap
/ɒ/	not	/dʒ/	job
/ɔː/	four	/f/	food
/ʊ/	look	/v/	very
/uː/	you	/θ/	think
/ə/	sugar	/ð/	then
/ʌ/	mum	/s/	speak
/eɪ/	day	/z/	zoo
/aɪ/	why	/ʃ/	she
/ɔɪ/	boy	/ʒ/	television
/aʊ/	how	/h/	hat
/əʊ/	go	/m/	meat
/ɪə/	ear	/n/	now
/eə/	wear	/ŋ/	sing
/ʊə/	tourist	/l/	late
		/r/	red
		/j/	yes
		/w/	we

Unit 1

Word stress: noun endings

1 4.11 **Listen. Match the words and the stress patterns. Then listen and repeat.**

argument
1 community
2 situation
3 collection
4 university
5 treatment

●•
●••
•●•
•●••
••●•
••●••

2 4.12 **Write the stress patterns for the words. Then listen, check and repeat.**

activity •●••
1 argument ●••
2 collection •●•
3 entertainment ••●•
4 location •●•
5 possibility ••●••
6 quality ●••
7 reaction •●•
8 situation ••●•
9 treatment ●•

Unit 2

Past simple endings: /d/, /t/, /ɪd/

1 4.13 **Listen and repeat. Listen to the last sounds in the words.**

/d/	/t/	/ɪd/
snowed	walked	chatted
played	jumped	decided

2 4.14 **Listen. What final sounds do you hear? Write d, t or ɪd. Then listen, check and repeat.**

phoned d
1 finished t
2 dived d
3 watched t
4 needed ɪd
5 danced t
6 tidied d
7 crawled d
8 shouted ɪd
9 liked t
10 climbed d

Unit 3

Sentence stress

1 4.15 **Listen and repeat. Listen to the stressed syllables.**

Look! ●
Wake up! ● ●
She laughed. • ●
Don't worry! ● ● •
I was talking. • • ● •
What were you doing? ● • • ● •
She shouted loudly. • ● • ● •
See you tomorrow! ● • • ● •

2 4.16 **Listen. Match the sentences with the same stress patterns.**

Stop! *c)*
1 Taxi! e)
2 She sings well. b)
3 Were you cross? a)
4 Was he waiting? f)
5 What was he thinking? d)

a) I'm the best.
b) We worked hard.
c) Help!
d) Why are they smiling?
e) Careful!
f) They were laughing.

3 4.17 **Listen and check.**

Unit 4

/ɔː/ v /ɜː/

1 4.18 **Listen and repeat.**

/ɔː/	/ɜː/
bored	bird

2 4.19 **Listen. Circle the words you hear. Then listen and repeat.**

short / (shirt)
1 wore / (were)
2 (born) / burn
3 (walk) / work
4 (talk) / Turk
5 (export) / expert

3 4.20 **Listen and repeat.**

She walks to work.
He wore a shirt.
They were short.
The expert was bored.
We learned to surf.
I was born on Thursday the first.

Unit 5

Stress in adjectives

1 4.21 **Listen and repeat.**

Two syllables	Three syllables	Four syllables
cheerful ● •	talkative ● • •	intelligent • ● • •
reserved • ●	ambitious • ● •	optimistic • • ● •

2 4.22 **Listen. Put the words in the correct columns.**

~~beautiful~~ confident correct entertainment funny horizontal modest pessimistic ridiculous selfish successful

1 ● •	3 ● • •	5 • ● • •
funny	beautiful	ridiculous
modest	confident	
selfish		
2 • ●	**4 • ● •**	**6 • • ● •**
correct	successful	entertainment
		horizontal
		pessimistic

3 4.23 **Listen and check. Then repeat.**

Unit 6

Weak forms

1 4.24 **Listen and repeat. Listen to the unstressed words.**

Nick has gone. That was the boy.
Tom and I have finished. I can ski.
Come to the party.

2 4.25 **Listen. How many words are not there? Write 0, 1 or 2.**

They're ... USA. 2
1 We ... late. 1
2 Look ... brother. 2
3 Go ... home. 0
4 I'm ... new teacher. 1
5 Stand ... up. 0
6 Who ... with? 2

3 4.26 **Listen again and complete the sentences. Then listen and repeat.**

They're from the USA.
1 We were ______ late.
2 Look at your ______ brother.
3 Go ______ home.
4 I'm your ______ new teacher.
5 Stand ______ up.
6 Who were you ______ with?

Unit 7

/əʊ/

1 4.27 **Listen and repeat.**

phone old road toe slow

2 4.28 **Listen and circle the words with vowel sounds that do not match. Then listen and repeat.**

only own (out) over
1 poem Joe (shoe) goes
2 (store) note wrote phone
3 snow show know (now)
4 clothes (other) both road
5 most post (cost) toast
6 coat spoke boat (come)

Unit 8

Contractions

1 4.29 **Listen and repeat.**

You won. You've won.
I love to go. I'd love to go.
I could come. I couldn't come.
They play. They'll play.

2 4.30 **Listen. Circle the sentences you hear.**

You like this. (You'll like this.)
1 (They want to leave.) They won't leave.
2 We'll speak English. (We speak English.)
3 (She could teach.) She couldn't teach.
4 They like to see you. (They'd like to see you.)
5 Mark is talking. (Mark isn't talking.)
6 (I've found it.) I found it.

Unit 9

Intonation in questions

1 4.31 **Listen and repeat.**

Rising

Is it made in Spain?
Will you be at the party?
Have they been shopping?

Falling

What were you doing?
How long has she lived here?
Why was he late?

2 4.32 **Listen. Does the intonation rise or fall? Write R or F. Then listen and repeat.**

Have you seen him? R
1 Where is it made? F
2 Who will be at the party? F
3 Would you like to go? R
4 Was he waiting? R
5 When will he arrive? F
6 Did you make this pizza? R

Word Bank

A

a few /ə 'fju:/ varios
a lot (of) /ə 'lɒt/ un montón (de)
about to /ə'baʊt tu:/ a punto de
above /ə'bʌv/ sobre
accept /ək'sept/ aceptar
according to /ə'kɔ:dɪŋ tu:/ según
act /ækt/ actuar
actually /'æktʃuəli/ de hecho, en realidad
address /ə'dres/ dirección
admit /æd'mɪt/ reconocer
adventurous /əd'ventʃərəs/ aventurero, intrépido
advertisement /ad/ /əd'vɜ:tɪsment/ /æd/ anuncio
advertising /'ædvətaɪzɪŋ/ publicidad
advice /əd'vaɪs/ consejo(s)
aeroplane /'eərəpleɪn/ avión
afterwards /'ɑ:ftəwədz/ después
again /ə'gen, ə'geɪn/ otra vez
age /eɪdʒ/ edad
ago /ə'gəʊ/ hace
agree /ə'gri:/ estar de acuerdo
aircraft /'eəkrɑ:ft/ avión
airport /'eəpɔ:t/ aeropuerto
album /'ælbəm/ álbum, disco
all /ɔ:l/ todos
allow /ə'laʊ/ dejar
almost /'ɔ:lməʊst/ casi
alone /ə'ləʊn/ solo
along /ə'lɒŋ/ por, a lo largo
also /'ɔ:lsəʊ/ también
although /ɔ:l'ðəʊ/ aunque
always /'ɔ:lweɪz/ siempre
amazing /ə'meɪzɪŋ/ asombroso
ambulance /'æmbjuləns/ ambulancia
amusement arcade /ə'mju:zmənt ɑ:keɪd/ salón de juegos
angle /'æŋgl/ ángulo
angry /'æŋgri/ enfadado
annoyed /ə'nɔɪd/ enfadado
another /ə'nʌðə/ otro
answer /'ɑ:nsə/ respuesta
anxious /'æŋkʃəs/ nervioso
anything /'eniθɪŋ/ algo, nada
anywhere /'eniweə/ en cualquier sitio
appear /ə'pɪə/ aparecer
appearance /ə'pɪərəns/ aspecto
applaud /ə'plɔ:d/ aplaudir
applause /ə'plɔ:z/ aplauso
apple /'æpl/ manzana
appliance /ə'plaɪəns/ aparato
argue /'ɑ:gju:/ discutir
armchair /'ɑ:mtʃeə/ butaca
around /ə'raʊnd/ alrededor
arrest /ə'rest/ detener
arrive /ə'raɪv/ llegar
arson /'ɑ:sn/ incendio provocado
art /ɑ:t/ plástica
article /'ɑ:tɪkl/ artículo
as usual /əz 'ju:ʒuəl, əz 'ju:ʒəl/ como siempre
assassinate /ə'sæsɪneɪt/ asesinar a una persona relevante
at all /ət 'ɔ:l/ en absoluto, nada
at first /ət 'fɜ:st/ al principio
attach /ə'tætʃ/ adjuntar
attack /ə'tæk/ ataque
attitude /'ætɪtju:d/ actitud
attract /ə'trækt/ atraer
aunt /ɑ:nt/ tía
autumn /'ɔ:təm/ otoño
average /'ævərɪdʒ/ medio
awake /ə'weɪk/ despierto
away from /ə'weɪ frɒm/ lejos de

B

baby /'beɪbi/ bebé
back /bæk/ respaldo
(at the) back /bæk/ detrás
backwards /'bækwədz/ hacia atrás
(feel) bad /bæd/ (sentirse) mal
badly /'bædli/ mal
bad-tempered /bæd'tempəd/ de mal genio, humor
bag /bæg/ bolsa
baggy /'bægi/ ancho
baker's /'beɪkəz/ panadería
ban /bæn/ prohibición, prohibir
banana /bə'nɑ:nə/ plátano
band /bænd/ grupo de música
bandage /'bændɪdʒ/ vendaje
bank /bæŋk/ banco
bank account /'bæŋk əkaʊnt/ cuenta bancaria
barbecue /'bɑ:bɪkju:/ barbacoa
BASE jumping /'beɪs dʒʌmpɪŋ/ salto con paracaídas desde edificios, montañas y puentes
basement /'beɪsmənt/ sótano
basket /'bɑ:skɪt/ cesto, cesta
basketball /'bɑ:skɪtbɔ:l/ baloncesto
bathroom /'bɑ:θru:m, 'bɑ:θrʊm/ cuarto de baño
battle /'bætl/ batalla
be born /bi 'bɔ:n/ nacer
be careful /bi 'keəfl/ tener cuidado
be keen on /bi 'ki:n ɒn/ gustar
be out /bi 'aʊt/ estar fuera
be out (with friends) /bi 'aʊt/ haber salido con amigos
be right /bi 'raɪt/ tener razón
be stuck /bi 'stʌk/ estar atrapado
be worth /bi 'wɜ:θ/ merecer la pena
beach /bi:tʃ/ playa
bean /bi:n/ judía
beautiful /'bju:tɪfl/ precioso
beauty /'bju:ti/ hermosura
because /bɪ'kɒz/ porque
because of /bɪ'kɒz əv/ debido a
bed /bed/ cama
bedroom /'bedru:m, 'bedrʊm/ habitación, dormitorio
bed-side table /bedsaɪd 'teɪbl/ mesilla
beef /bi:f/ (carne de) ternera
before /bɪ'fɔ:/ antes (de)
begin /bɪ'gɪn/ empezar
behave /bɪ'heɪv/ comportarse
behind /bɪ'haɪnd/ detrás (de)
believe /bɪ'li:v/ creer
below /bɪ'ləʊ/ (por) debajo de
bench /bentʃ/ banco
bend /bend/ curva
bend down /bend 'daʊn/ agacharse
best /best/ (el) mejor
bet /bet/ apostar
better /'betə/ mejor
between /bɪ'twi:n/ entre
big /bɪg/ grande
big-headed /bɪg'hedɪd/ chulo, engreído
bike /baɪk/ bici
bin /bɪn/ cubo de basura
biology /baɪ'ɒlədʒi/ biología
birthday /'bɜ:θdeɪ/ cumpleaños
biscuit /'bɪskɪt/ galleta
blank /blæŋk/ en blanco, vacío
blow /bləʊ/ soplar, sonar
blunt /blʌnt/ afilado
body /'bɒdi/ cuerpo
boil /bɔɪl/ hervir
bone /bəʊn/ hueso
book /bʊk/ reservar
bookshop /'bʊkʃɒp/ librería
bored /bɔ:d/ aburrido
boring /'bɔ:rɪŋ/ aburrido, que aburre
borrow /'bɒrəʊ/ tomar prestado
boss /bɒs/ jefe, jefa
bottle /'bɒtl/ botella
box /bɒks/ caja
boyfriend /'bɔɪfrend/ novio
brave /breɪv/ valiente
bread /bred/ pan
break /breɪk/ descanso
break into /breɪk 'ɪntu:/ entrar (por la fuerza) en
break the law /breɪk ðə 'lɔ:/ romper la ley
breakfast /'brekfəst/ desayuno
breathing /'bri:ðɪŋ/ respiración
bridge /brɪdʒ/ puente
brightly /'braɪtli/ brillante, con fuerza
brilliant /'brɪliənt/ genial
bring /brɪŋ/ traer
broadband /'brɔ:dbænd/ banda ancha
broad-shouldered /brɔ:d'ʃəʊldəd/ ancho de espalda
broken arm /brəʊkn 'ɑ:m/ brazo roto
brother /'brʌðə/ hermano
build /bɪld/ construir
builder /'bɪldə/ obrero, obrera de la construcción
building /'bɪldɪŋ/ edificio
bullet /'bʊlɪt/ bala
bungee jumping /'bʌndʒi dʒʌmpɪŋ/ puenting
burger /'bɜ:gə/ hamburguesa
burglary /'bɜ:gləri/ robo
burn /bɜ:n/ quemar
bush /bʊʃ/ arbusto
business woman /'bɪznəs wʊmən/ mujer de negocios
businessman /'bɪznəsmæn, 'bɪznəsmən/ hombre de negocios
busy /'bɪzi/ ocupado
but /bʌt/ pero
butcher's /'bʊtʃəz/ carnicería
butter /'bʌtə/ mantequilla
buy /baɪ/ comprar
(by) bus /bʌs/ (en) autobús

C

cake /keɪk/ tarta
calculation /kælkju'leɪʃn/ cáculo, operación
call /kɔ:l/ llamar
camcorder /'kæmkɔ:də/ cámara de vídeo
camp /kæmp/ campamento
campaigner /kæm'peɪnə/ defensor, defensora
can /kæn/ lata
candle /'kændl/ vela
cap /kæp/ gorra
car /kɑ:/ coche
card /kɑ:d/ tarjeta, postal
care /keə/ cuidado
career /kə'rɪə/ trayectoria profesional
careful /'keəfl/ cuidadoso
carpet /'kɑ:pɪt/ moqueta
carrier bag /'kæriə bæg/ bolsa de plástico
carrot /'kærət/ zanahoria
carry /'kæri/ llevar
carton /'kɑ:tn/ cartón
case /keɪs/ caso
cash /kæʃ/ dinero en metálico
cashier /kə'ʃɪə/ cajero, cajera
casual /'kæʒuəl/ informal
cause /kɔ:z/ porque
caving /'keɪvɪŋ/ espeleología
ceiling /'si:lɪŋ/ techo
celebrate /'selɪbreɪt/ celebrar
celebrity /sə'lebrəti/ persona famosa
cell /sel/ celda
centre /'sentə/ centro
century /'sentʃəri/ siglo
certain /'sɜ:tn/ cierto
certainly /'sɜ:tnli/ por supuesto
chalk /tʃɔ:k/ tiza
champagne /ʃæm'peɪn/ champán
chance /tʃɑ:ns/ oportunidad
change /tʃeɪndʒ/ cambiar, cambio
channel /'tʃænl/ canal
character /'kærəktə/ personaje
charge /tʃɑ:dʒ/ cobrar
chat /tʃæt/ charlar, chatear
chat room /'tʃæt ru:m, 'tʃæt rʊm/ zona de chateo
cheat /tʃi:t/ tramposo, tramposa
check /tʃek/ comprobar
check-out /'tʃekaʊt/ caja
cheerful /'tʃɪəfl/ alegre
cheese /tʃi:z/ queso
cheetah /'tʃi:tə/ guepardo
chemist's /'kemɪsts/ farmacia
chemistry /'kemɪstri/ química
chess /tʃes/ ajedrez
chest of drawers /tʃest əv 'drɔ:z/ cómoda
chewing gum /'tʃu:ɪŋ gʌm/ chicle
chicken /'tʃɪkɪn/ pollo
child /children /tʃaɪld/ /'tʃɪldrən/ niño, niña / niños, niñas
chimney /'tʃɪmni/ chimenea
chips /tʃɪps/ patatas fritas
choice /tʃɔɪs/ elección
choose /tʃu:z/ escoger
Christmas /'krɪsməs/ Navidad

church /tʃɜ:tʃ/ iglesia
cider /'saɪdə/ sidra
cigar /sɪ'gɑ:/ (cigarro) puro
cinema /'sɪnəmə/ cine
civil rights /sɪvl 'raɪts/ derechos civiles
claim /kleɪm/ decir, afirmar
class /klɑ:s/ clase
classical music /klæsɪkl 'mju:zɪk/ música clásica
clean /kli:n/ limpio
cliff /klɪf/ acantilado
climb /klaɪm/ trepar, escalar
cloak /kləʊk/ capa
close /kləʊs/ cerca
clothes /kləʊðz/ ropa
clothing /'kləʊðɪŋ/ ropa
cloud /klaʊd/ nube
clue /klu:/ pista
clumsy /'klʌmzi/ torpe
coat /kəʊt/ chaquetón
coffee /'kɒfi/ café
cold /kəʊld/ frío
collect /kəlekt/ coleccionar
college /'kɒlɪdʒ/ universidad
come /kʌm/ venir
come in /kʌm 'ɪn/ entrar
comfortable /'kʌmftəbl/ cómodo
comfy /'kʌmfi/ cómodo
comic /'kɒmɪk/ cómic, tebeo
commit /kə'mɪt/ cometer
common /'kɒmən/ común, frecuente
communicate /kə'mju:nɪkeɪt/ comunicarse
community /kə'mju:nəti/ comunidad
company /'kʌmpəni/ compañía
compass /'kʌmpəs/ brújula
complexion /kəm'plekʃn/ piel
compress /'kɒmpres/ comprimir
computer /kəm'pju:tə/ ordenador
computer studies /kəm'pju:tə stʌdiz/ informática
concert /'kɒnsət/ concierto
conference /'kɒnfərəns/ congreso
confident /'kɒnfɪdənt/ seguro de sí mismo
confused /kən'fju:zd/ confuso
connect /kə'nekt/ conectar
constantly /'kɒnstəntli/ constantemente
construction worker /kən'strʌkʃn wɜ:kə/ trabajador, trabajadora de la construcción
consume /kən'sju:m/ consumir
contain /kən'teɪn/ contener
container /kən'teɪnə/ recipiente, envase
contestant /kən'testənt/ concursante
continue /kən'tɪnju:/ seguir, continuar
cook /kʊk/ cocinar, cocinero, cocinera
cooker /'kʊkə/ cocina (electrodoméstico)
cool /ku:l/ guay
copy /'kɒpi/ copiar, copia
corner /'kɔ:nə/ esquina
cost /kɒst/ costar
costume /'kɒstju:m/ traje
counter /'kaʊntə/ barra, mostrador
country /'kʌntri/ país
(a) couple (of) /'kʌpl/ (un) par (de)
court /kɔ:t/ juzgado
cous cous /kʊs kʊs, ku:s ku:s/ cuscús
cousin /'kʌzn/ primo, prima
cover /'kʌvə/ cubrir, abarcar
cow /kaʊ/ vaca
crawl /krɔ:l/ arrastrarse
cream /kri:m/ nata
crime /kraɪm/ delito, crimen
cross /krɒs/ enfadado, cruzar
cup /kʌp/ taza
cupboard /'kʌbəd/ armario
curly /'kɜ:li/ rizado
currency /'kʌrənsi/ moneda
current /'kʌrənt/ actual
custard /'kʌstəd/ crema, natillas
customer /'kʌstəmə/ cliente, clienta
cycle /'saɪkl/ andar en bici

D

damage /'dæmɪdʒ/ afectar a, dañar
dance /dɑ:ns/ bailar, baile
danger /'deɪndʒə/ peligro
dark /dɑ:k/ oscuro
database /'deɪtəbeɪs/ base de datos
date (back) /deɪt/ remontarse
day /deɪ/ día
debt /det/ deuda
decide /dɪ'saɪd/ decidir
deduction /dɪ'dʌkʃn/ deducción
deep /di:p/ profundo
deerstalker hat /dɪəstɔ:kə 'hæt/ gorro de cazador
definitely /'defɪnətli/ sin duda
definition /defɪ'nɪʃn/ definición
degree /dɪ'gri:/ grado
delighted /dɪ'laɪtɪd/ encantado
demonstration /demən'streɪʃn/ manifestación
desert /'dezət/ desierto
deserve /dɪ'zɜ:v/ merecer
desire /dɪ'zaɪə/ deseo
desk /desk/ mesa, escritorio
dessert /dɪ'zɜ:t/ postre
destroy /dɪ'strɔɪ/ destruir
details /'di:teɪlz/ detalles
detective story /dɪ'tektɪv stɔ:ri/ novela policiaca
develop /dɪ'veləp/ desarrollar
device /dɪ'vaɪs/ aparato
devil /'devl/ diablo
die /daɪ/ morir
dinner /'dɪnə/ cena
dirty /'dɜ:ti/ sucio
disagree /dɪsə'gri:/ no estar de acuerdo
disappointed /dɪsə'pɔɪntɪd/ decepcionado
disc drive /'dɪsk draɪv/ unidad de disco
discount /'dɪskaʊnt/ descuento
discover /dɪ'skʌvə/ descubrir
disease /dɪ'zi:z/ enfermedad
disgusting /dɪs'gʌstɪŋ/ asqueroso
district /'dɪstrɪkt/ distrito
dive /daɪv/ bucear
dizzy /'dɪzi/ mareado
do /du:/ hacer
do crafts /du: 'krɑ:fts/ hacer trabajos manuales
do gymnastics /du: dʒɪm'næstɪks/ hacer gimnasia
do the dusting /du: ðə 'dʌstɪŋ/ quitar el polvo
do the gardening /du: ðə 'gɑ:dnɪŋ/ cuidar el jardín
do the hoovering /du: ðə hu:vərɪŋ/ pasar el aspirador
do the ironing /du: ði 'aɪənɪŋ/ planchar
do the shopping /du: ðə 'ʃɒpɪŋ/ hacer la compra
do the washing /du: ðə 'wɒʃɪŋ/ hacer la colada
doctor /'dɒktə/ médico, médica
dog /dɒg/ perro
dollar /'dɒlə/ dólar
donate /dəʊ'neɪt/ donar
donor /'dəʊnə/ donante
door /dɔ:/ puerta
download /daʊn'ləʊd/ descargar
drama /'drɑ:mə/ teatro
draw /drɔ:/ dibujar
dream /dri:m/ sueño
dress /dres/ vestido
dress up /dres 'ʌp/ disfrazarse
drink /drɪŋk/ bebida
drive /draɪv/ conducir
drop /drɒp/ dejar caer, bajar
drug /drʌg/ droga, medicina
drug dealing /'drʌg di:lɪŋ/ tráfico de drogas
(the) drums /drʌmz/ (la) batería
dry /draɪ/ secar, seco
during /'djʊərɪŋ/ durante
dustbin /'dʌstbɪn/ cubo de basura

E

each /i:tʃ/ cada
ear /ɪə/ oreja
early /'ɜ:li/ temprano
earn /ɜ:n/ ganar (dinero)
Earth /ɜ:θ/ Tierra
easy /'i:zi/ fácil
easy-going /i:zi'gəʊɪŋ/ tranquilo, de buen carácter
eat /i:t/ comer
egg white /'eg waɪt/ clara de huevo
egg yolk /'eg jəʊk/ yema de huevo
embarrassed /ɪm'bærəst/ avergonzado
emphasize /'emfəsaɪz/ enfatizar
employ /ɪm'plɔɪ/ emplear
end /end/ final
enemy /enəmi/ enemigo, enemiga
energy /'enədʒi/ energía
engine /'endʒɪn/ máquina
enjoy /ɪn'dʒɔɪ/ disfrutar de, pasarlo bien
enormous /ɪ'nɔ:məs/ enorme
enough /ɪ'nʌf/ suficiente, suficientes
enter /'entə/ introducir, participar en (una competición)
entertain /entə'teɪn/ entretener
equator /ɪ'kweɪtə/ ecuador
equipment /ɪ'kwɪpmənt/ material
escape /ɪ'skeɪp/ escapar
essay /'eseɪ/ redacción
estate agent's /ɪ'steɪt eɪdʒənts/ kiosco
event /ɪ'vent/ acto, celebración
eventually /ɪ'ventʃuəli/ al final
every /'evri/ cada, todos los
everything /'evriθɪŋ/ todo
evidence /'evɪdəns/ testimonio, muestra
example /ɪg'zɑ:mpl/ ejemplo
exchange /ɪks'tʃeɪndʒ/ intercambiar
(be) excited /ɪk'saɪtɪd/ alterarse, ponerse nervioso
exciting /ɪk'saɪtɪŋ/ emocionante
execute /'eksɪkjut/ ejecutar
exhausted /ɪg'zɔ:stɪd/ agotado
exit /'egzɪt/ salida
expect /ɪk'spekt/ esperar
expensive /ɪk'spensɪv/ caro
explain /ɪk'spleɪn/ explicar
extract /'ekstrækt/ fragmento
extreme sport /ɪkstri:m 'spɔ:t/ deporte extremo
extremely /ɪk'stri:mli/ extremadamente, muy
eye /aɪ/ ojo

F

fabric /'fæbrɪk/ tela
face /feɪs/ enfrentarse a, cara, rostro
fact /fækt/ hecho
factory /'fæktri/ fábrica
fail /feɪl/ fracasar, suspender
fair /feə/ claro, rubio
fall off /fɔ:l 'ɒf/ caerse (de)
fame /feɪm/ fama
fancy /'fænsi/ elegante
far /fɑ:/ lejos
farm /fɑ:m/ granja
fashion /'fæʃn/ moda
fast /fɑ:st/ rápido
fat /fæt/ grasa
fatty /'fæti/ graso
fault /fɔ:lt/ culpa
fearless /'fɪələs/ intrépido
feather /'feðə/ pluma
fed up /fed 'ʌp/ harto
feel /fi:l/ sentirse
feel like /'fi:l laɪk/ apetecer
female /'fi:meɪl/ mujer, chica
fence /fens/ valla
field /fi:ld/ campo
fight /faɪt/ lucha, pelea, luchar, pelear
film /fɪlm/ película
find /faɪnd/ encontrar
finger /'fɪŋgə/ dedo
fingerprint /'fɪŋgəprɪnt/ huella digital
finish /'fɪnɪʃ/ acabar
fire /faɪə/ fuego, disparar
first /fɜ:st/ primer
first aid /fɜ:st 'eɪd/ primeros auxilios
first-aid kit /fɜ:st'eɪd kɪt/ botiquín
fish /fɪʃ/ pez

fish and chips /fɪʃ n 'tʃɪps/ pescado rebozado con patatas fritas
fit /fɪt/ en forma, quedar, sentar bien
fix /fɪks/ arreglar
flat /flæt/ piso
flavour /'fleɪvə/ sabor
flight /flaɪt/ vuelo
floor /flɔ:/ suelo, piso
flour /'flaʊə/ harina
flower /'flaʊə/ flor
flower bed /'flaʊə bed/ parterre
folks /fəʊks/ tipos
follow /'fɒləʊ/ seguir
food /fu:d/ comida
forest /'fɒrɪst/ bosque
forget /fə'get/ olvidar
form /fɔ:m/ forma
forwards /'fɔ:wədz/ hacia adelante
free /fri:/ libre, liberar
free running /fri: 'rʌnɪŋ/ acrobacias urbanas
free time /fri: 'taɪm/ tiempo libre
freeze /fri:z/ congelar
fresh /freʃ/ fresco
fried egg /fraɪd'eg/ huevo frito
friend /frend/ amigo, amiga
friendly /'frendli/ amable
frightened /'fraɪtnd/ asustado
front door /frʌnt 'dɔ:/ puerta principal
fruit /fru:t/ fruta(s)
FTP site /efti:'pi: saɪt/ sitio FTP
full of /'fʊl əv/ lleno de
fun /fʌn/ divertido
funny /'fʌni/ gracioso
furniture /'fɜ:nɪtʃə/ muebles
further /'fɜ:ðə/ más lejos
furthermore /fɜ:ðə'mɔ:/ lo que es más

G

gadget /'gædʒɪt/ artilugios, chismes
gang /gæŋ/ banda
gap year /'gæp jɪə/ año libre (antes de ir a la universidad)
garden /'gɑ:dn/ jardín
gentleman /'dʒentlmən/ caballero
geography /dʒi:'ɒgrəfi/ geografía
get /get/ conseguir
get bigger /get 'bɪgə/ aumentar de tamaño
get fatter /get 'fætə/ engordar
get lost /get 'lɒst/ perderse
get married /get 'mærid/ casarse
get off /get 'ɒf/ bajar (de)
get out /get 'aʊt/ salir
get up /get 'ʌp/ levantarse
get upset /get ʌp'set/ disgustarse
girl /gɜ:l/ chica
give /gɪv/ dar
give away /gɪv ə'weɪ/ regalar
give back /gɪv 'bæk/ devolver
give in /gɪv 'ɪn/ entregar
give out /gɪv 'aʊt/ repartir
give up /gɪv 'ʌp/ dejar, ceder
glass /glɑ:s/ vaso
glasses /'glɑ:sɪz/ gafas
global warming /gləʊbl 'wɔ:mɪŋ/ calentamiento del planeta
gloves /glʌvz/ guantes
glue /glu:/ pegamento, cola
go /gəʊ/ ir
go bowling /gəʊ 'bəʊlɪŋ/ juegar a los bolos
go camping /gəʊ 'kæmpɪŋ/ ir de acampada
go down /gəʊ 'daʊn/ bajar
go horseriding /gəʊ 'hɔ:sraɪdɪŋ/ montar a caballo
go jogging /gəʊ 'dʒɒgɪŋ/ ir a correr
go out /gəʊ 'aʊt/ salir
go to bed /gəʊ tə 'bed/ acostarse
go to sleep /gəʊ tə 'sli:p/ dormirse
go up /gəʊ 'ʌp/ subir
go wrong /gəʊ 'rɒŋ/ salir mal
goal /gəʊl/ objetivo
gold /gəʊld/ oro
good /gʊd/ bueno
government /'gʌvənmənt/ gobierno
graceful /'greɪsfl/ grácil, elegante
grandad /'grændæd/ abuelo, abuelito
grandparent /'grænpeərənt/ abuelo o abuela
grass court /grɑ:s 'kɔ:t/ pista de hierba
great /greɪt/ grande, genial
greedily /'grɪ:dɪli/ con avidez
green bean /gri:n 'bi:n/ judía verde
ground /graʊnd/ suelo
grow /grəʊ/ crecer, aumentar
guess /ges/ adivinar
guest /gest/ invitado, invitada
guide /gaɪd/ guía
guilty /'gilti/ culpable
gun /gʌn/ pistola

H

hacking /'hækɪŋ/ piratería informática
hair /heə/ pelo
hair gel /'heə dʒel/ gomina
haircut /'heəkʌt/ corte de pelo
hairdresser's /'heədresəz/ peluquería
half /hɑ:f/ medio, mitad
hall /hɔ:l/ hall, entrada
ham /hæm/ jamón
(by) hand /hænd/ (a) mano
handcuffs /'hændkʌfs/ esposas
handwriting /'hændraɪtɪŋ/ letra, escritura
hang-gliding /'hæŋ glaɪdɪŋ/ ala delta
happen /'hæpn/ ocurrir
happy /'hæpi/ contento, feliz
hard drive /'hɑ:d draɪv/ disco duro
hardly ever /hɑ:dli 'evə/ casi nunca
hard-working /hɑ:d 'wɜ:kɪŋ/ trabajador
harm /hɑ:m/ daño
hat /hæt/ sombrero
hate /heɪt/ odiar
have /hæv/ tener
have a bath /hæv ə 'bɑ:θ/ darse un baño
have a meal out /hæv ə mi:l 'aʊt/ salir a comer/cenar
have to /hæv 'tu:/ tener que
head teacher /hed 'ti:tʃə/ director, directora de escuela
headache /'hedeɪk/ dolor de cabeza
healing /'hi:lɪŋ/ curación
healthy /'helθi/ saludable, sano
hear /hɪə/ oír, escuchar
heart /hɑ:t/ corazón
heart disease /'hɑ:t dɪzi:z/ cardiopatía
heat /hi:t/ calentar
heavy /'hevi/ pesado, (lluvia) intensa
hedge /hedʒ/ seto
height /haɪt/ altura
helmet /'helmɪt/ casco
help /help/ ayudar, ayuda
here /hɪə/ aquí
hi /haɪ/ hola
hide /haɪd/ esconderse
hi-fi /'haɪfaɪ/ equipo de música
high /haɪ/ alto
high heel /haɪ 'hi:l/ tacón
high school /'haɪ sku:l/ instituto
high street /'haɪ stri:t/ calle principal
hiking /'haɪkɪŋ/ excursionismo
hill /hɪl/ colina
holiday /'hɒlɪdeɪ/ vacaciones
(at) home /həʊm/ (en) casa
homeless /'həʊmləs/ sin techo
homework /'həʊmwɜ:k/ deberes
hope (to) /həʊp/ esperar
hose /həʊz/ manguera
hostel /'hɒstl/ albergue
hot /hɒt/ caliente
hour /'aʊə/ hora
house /haʊs/ casa
housework /'haʊswɜ:k/ tareas domésticas
how /haʊ/ ¿cómo?
how long? /haʊ 'lɒŋ/ ¿cuánto tiempo?
how much? /haʊ 'mʌtʃ/ ¿cuánto?
how tall? /haʊ 'tɔ:l/ ¿qué altura?
however /haʊ'evə/ sin embargo
huge /hju:dʒ/ enorme
hundred /'hʌndrəd/ cien
hungry /'hʌŋgri/ hambriento
hurry /'hʌri/ darse prisa
husband /'hʌzbənd/ marido

I

ice cream /aɪs 'kri:m, 'aɪs kri:m/ helado
icy /'aɪsi/ helado
ill /ɪl/ enfermo
image /'ɪmɪdʒ/ imagen
imagine /ɪ'mædʒɪn/ imaginarse
immediately /ɪ'mi:diətli/ inmediatamente
important /ɪm'pɔ:tnt/ importante
improvement /ɪm'pru:vmənt/ mejora
in addition /ɪn ə'dɪʃn/ además
in between /ɪn bɪ'twi:n/ entre uno y otro
in fact /ɪn 'fækt/ de hecho
in love /ɪn 'lʌv/ enamorado
in trouble /ɪn 'trʌbl/ (tener) problemas
include /ɪn'klu:d/ incluir
increase /ɪn'kri:s/ aumentar, aumento
influential /ɪnflu'enʃl/' influyente
inhabitant /ɪn'hæbɪtənt/ habitante
injure /'ɪndʒə/ lesionarse
ink /ɪnk/ tinta
inside /ɪn'saɪd/ dentro
instead /ɪn'sted/ en lugar de eso
insulate /'ɪnsjəleɪt/ aislar
insurance company /ɪn'ʃʊərəns kʌmpəni/ compañía de seguros
interesting /'ɪntrəstɪŋ/ interesante
into /'ɪntu:/ dentro de
iron /'aɪən/ planchar
ironing board /'aɪənɪŋ bɔ:d/ tabla para la plancha
island /'aɪlənd/ isla
issue /'ɪsju:/ tema
item /'aɪtəm/ artículo

J

jacket /'dʒækɪt/ chaqueta
jam /dʒæm/ mermelada
jar /dʒɑ:/ frasco, tarro
jealous /'dʒeləs/ celoso
jelly /'dʒeli/ gelatina
jewellery shop /'dʒu:əlri ʃɒp/ joyería
job /dʒɒb/ trabajo
join /dʒɔɪn/ unirse a
journalist /'dʒɜ:nəlɪst/ periodista
joyriding /'dʒɔɪraɪdɪŋ/ robar automóviles por diversión
judge /dʒʌdʒ/ juzgar, juez, jueza
juggling /'dʒʌglɪŋ/ malabares
juice /dʒu:s/ zumo
jump /dʒʌmp/ saltar, salto
jumper /'dʒʌmpə/ jersey
junk food /'dʒʌŋk fu:d/ comida basura
jury /dʒʊəri/ jurado
just /dʒʌst/ simplemente, solo

K

keep /ki:p/ conservar
keep a record /ki:p ə 'rekɔ:d/ tomar nota
kettle /'ketl/ hervidora eléctrica
key /ki:/ llave, clave
kidney /'kɪdni/ riñón
kill /kɪl/ matar
kill off /kɪl 'ɒf/ eliminar
kind /kaɪnd/ tipo
kind-hearted /kaɪnd'hɑ:tɪd/ de buen corazón
king /kɪŋ/ rey
kiss /kɪs/ besar
kitchen /'kɪtʃɪn/ cocina
kite surfing /'kaɪt sɜ:fɪŋ/ volar cometas
knee /ni:/ rodilla
knife /naɪf/ cuchillo
knitting /'nɪtɪŋ/ hacer punto

knock /nɒk/ llamar, tocar
know /nəʊ/ saber

L

ladder /ˈlʌdə/ escalera
lake /leɪk/ lago
land /lænd/ (de) tierra, aterrizar
land area /ˈlænd eəriə/ zona terrestre
laptop /ˈlæptɒp/ portátil
large /lɑ:dʒ/ grande
last /lɑ:st/ pasado, último
last night /lɑ:st ˈnaɪt/ anoche
late /leɪt/ tarde
later /ˈleɪtə/ más tarde, después
laugh /lɑ:f/ reír(se)
law /lɔ:/ ley
lawn /lɔ:n/ césped
lawnmower /ˈlɔ:nməʊə/ cortacésped
lazy /ˈleɪzi/ vago
lead /li:d/ liderar
leaf, leaves /li:f/ /li:vz/ hoja, hojas
lean /li:n/ magro
learn /lɜ:n/ aprender
least /li:st/ (el) menos
leather /ˈleðə/ de cuero
leave /li:v/ marcharse (de)
left /left/ (a la) izquierda
leisure /ˈleʃə/ ocio
lend /lend/ prestar
less (than) /les/ menos (de)
let /let/ dejar
letter /ˈletə/ carta
lettuce /ˈletɪs/ lechuga
level /ˈlevl/ nivel
liar /ˈlaɪə/ mentiroso, mentirosa
library /ˈlaɪbrəri/ biblioteca
licence /ˈlaɪsəns/ permiso
life /laɪf/ vida
lifeguard /ˈlaifgɑ:d/ guardacostas
lift /lɪft/ llevar, acercar
light /laɪt/ luz
light bulb /ˈlaɪt bʌlb/ bombilla
like /laɪk/ gustar
likely /ˈlaɪkli/ probable
link /lɪŋk/ unir
lion /ˈlaɪən/ león
lips /lɪps/ labios
listen to /ˈlɪsn tu:/ escuchar
live /lɪv/ vivir
living room /ˈlɪvɪŋ ru:m, lɪvɪŋ rʊm/ sala de estar
load /ləʊd/ cargar
loads of /ˈləʊdz əv/ montones de
locate /ləʊˈkeɪt/ localizar
location /ləʊˈkeɪʃn/ localización
log onto /lɒg ˈɒntu:/ conectarse a
lonely /ˈləʊnli/ solo
long /lɒŋ/ largo
(be) long /lɒŋ/ durar
look /lʊk/ parecer, mirar
look after /lʊk ˈɑ:ftə/ cuidar a/de
look for /ˈlʊk fɔ:/ buscar
look forward to /lʊk ˈfɔ:wəd tu:/ estar deseando
look good /lʊk ˈgʊd/ tener buen aspecto
lorry /lɒri/ camión
lose /lu:z/ perder

loud /laʊd/ fuerte
love /lʌv/ con cariño
low /ləʊ/ bajo
loyal /ˈlɔɪəl/ leal
lucky /ˈlʌki/ afortunado
lunch /lʌntʃ/ comida (al mediodía)
lyrics /ˈlɪrɪks/ letra

M

magazine /mægəˈzi:n/ revista
main /meɪn/ principal
main course /meɪn ˈkɔ:s/ plato fuerte
mainland /ˈmeɪnlænd/ parte de un país que no incluye sus islas
make /meɪk/ hacer
make a mistake /meɪk ə mɪsˈteɪk/ cometer un error
make your bed /meɪk yə ˈbed/ hacer tu cama
male /meɪl/ hombre, chico
man (men) /mæn/ /men/ hombre (hombres)
mankind /mænˈkaɪnd/ humanidad
manufacturer /mænjuˈfæktʃərə/ fabricante
many /ˈmeni/ muchos
mark /mɑ:k/ corregir, nota
match /mætʃ/ partida
matches /ˈmætʃəz/ cerillas
mate /meɪt/ colega
maths /mæθs/ matemáticas
maybe /ˈmeɪbi:/ quizá
mayonnaise /meɪəˈneɪz/ mahonesa
meal /mi:l/ comida
mean /mi:n/ significar
meat /mi:t/ carne
medical /ˈmedɪkl/ médico
medicine /ˈmedsn, ˈmedɪsn/ medicina(s)
meet /mi:t/ conocer
member /ˈmembə/ miembro
memory stick /ˈmeməri stɪk/ lápiz de memoria
message /ˈmesɪdʒ/ mensaje
midday /mɪdˈdeɪ/ mediodía
middle /ˈmɪdl/ medio
middle-aged /mɪdl ˈeɪdʒd/ de mediana edad
milk /mɪlk/ leche
mind /maɪnd/ mente
mine /maɪn/ mío, míos
minority /maɪˈnɒrəti/ minoría
miserable /ˈmɪzrəbl/ triste
miss /mɪs/ perder(se)
mistake /mɪˈsteɪk/ error
mix /mɪks/ mezclar, mezcla
mobile phone recharger /məʊbaɪl ˈfəʊn ri:tʃɑ:dʒə/ cargador del móvil
money /ˈmʌni/ dinero
mood /mu:d/ humor
more (than) /mɔ:/ más (de)
most of /ˈməʊst ɒv/ la mayoría (de)
mostly /ˈməʊstli/ en su mayoría
mother /ˈmʌðə/ madre
motorbike /ˈməʊtəbaɪk/ moto
mountain /ˈmaʊntən/ montaña
moustache /məˈstɑ:ʃ/ bigote

move (around) /mu:v/ girar (alrededor de)
move /mu:v/ trasladarse
movie /ˈmu:vi/ película
MP3 dock /empi:ˈθri: dɒk/ microcadena MP3
MP3 player /empi:ˈθri: pleɪə/ reproductor de MP3
much /mʌtʃ/ mucho
mummy /ˈmʌmi/ mamá
murder /ˈmɜ:də/ asesinato
mushroom /ˈmʌʃrʊm, ˈmʌʃru:m/ champiñón
must /mʌst/ deber
(of) myself /maɪˈself/ mío
mystery /ˈmɪstri/ misterio

N

name /neɪm/ nombre
narrow /ˈnærəʊ/ estrecho
nasty /ˈnɑ:sti/ desagradable
nature /ˈneɪtʃə/ naturaleza
near /nɪə/ cerca de
need /ni:d/ necesitar
netbook /ˈnetbʊk/ miniordenador
never /ˈnevə/ nunca
new /nju:/ nuevo
news /nju:z/ noticias
newsagent's /ˈnju:zeɪdʒənts/ kiosco (de prensa)
newspaper /ˈnju:speɪpə/ periódico
next door /nekst ˈdɔə/ en la casa de al lado
nice /naɪs/ amable, agradable, rico
nickname /ˈnɪkneɪm/ apodo
(at) night /naɪt/ (de) noche
night club /ˈnaɪt klʌb/ discoteca
nobody /ˈnəʊbədi/ nadie
noise /nɔɪz/ ruido
notebook /ˈnəʊtbʊk/ cuaderno
notepad /ˈnəʊtpæd/ libreta
nothing /ˈnʌθɪŋ/ nada
notice /ˈnəʊtɪs/ fijarse (en)
notice board /ˈnəʊtɪs bɔ:d/ tablón de anuncios
now /naʊ/ ahora
nowadays /ˈnaʊədeɪz/ hoy en día
number /ˈnʌmbə/ número, cantidad

O

obviously /ˈɒbviəsli/ evidentemente
odd /ɒd/ raro
of course /əv ˈkɔ:s/ por supuesto
off /ɒf/ de
offer /ˈɒfə/ ofrecer
office /ˈɒfɪs/ oficina
often /ˈɒfn, ˈɒftən/ a menudo
old /əʊld/ viejo, antiguo
olive /ˈɒlɪv/ aceituna
omelette /ˈɒmlət/ tortilla
once /wʌns/ una vez
onion /ˈʌnjən/ cebolla
only /ˈəʊnli/ solo, solamente
onto /ˈɒntu:/ encima de
open /ˈəʊpn/ abrir
opposite /ˈɒpəzɪt/ contrario, opuesto
orchestra /ˈɔ:kestrə/ orquesta
order /ˈɔ:də/ encargar

orphan /ˈɔ:fn/ huérfano, huérfana
other /ˈʌðə/ otros
(be) out /aʊt/ (estar) fuera
(be) out and about /aʊt ənd ˈəbaʊt/ (salir) por ahí
out of /ˈaʊt ɒv/ fuera de
out of sight /aʊt əv ˈsaɪt/ escondido
outdoor /ˈaʊtdɔ:/ al aire libre
outfit /ˈaʊtfɪt/ traje, vestimenta
outgoing /ˈaʊtgəʊɪŋ/ sociable
outlaw /ˈaʊtlɔ:/ forajido, forajida
outside /aʊtˈsaɪd/ fuera (de)
over /ˈəʊvə/ más de
(all) over /ˈəʊvə/ por (todo)
overnight /əʊvəˈnaɪt/ por la noche
overweight /əʊvəˈweɪt/ gordo
owner /ˈəʊnə/ dueño, dueña

P

pack /pæk/ hacer la maleta
page /peɪdʒ/ página
paint /peɪnt/ pintura
pale /peɪl/ pálido
pan /pæn/ sartén
pancake /ˈpænkeɪk/ tortita
paper /ˈpeɪpə/ papel
parachuting /ˈpærəʃu:tɪŋ/ paracaidísimo
parents /ˈpeərənts/ padres (padre y madre)
park /pɑ:k/ parque
particularly /pəˈtɪkjələli/ sobre todo
partner /ˈpɑ:tnə/ pareja, compañero, compañera
party /ˈpɑ:ti/ fiesta
pass /pɑ:s/ aprobar, pasar (por)
passage /ˈpæsɪdʒ/ hueco
passenger /ˈpæsɪndʒə/ pasajero, pasajera
past /pɑ:st/ (del) pasado
path /pɑ:θ/ camino
pay /peɪ/ pagar
pay attention /peɪ əˈtenʃn/ prestar atención
pear /peə/ pera
peas /pi:z/ guisantes
pease-pudding /pi:zˈpʊdɪŋ/ tarta de guisantes
people /ˈpi:pl/ gente
pepper /ˈpepə/ pimiento, pimienta
perform /pəˈfɔ:m/ actuar
performer /pəˈfɔ:mə/ artista
performing arts /pəfɔ:mɪŋ ˈɑ:ts/ artes escénicas
period (of time) /ˈpɪəriəd/ periodo (de tiempo)
pet /pet/ mascota
photo /ˈfəʊtəʊ/ foto
physical /ˈfɪzɪkl/ físico
pick /pɪk/ recolectar
pick up /pɪkˈʌp/ recoger
picture /ˈpɪktʃə/ foto, imaginar
pie /paɪ/ pastel
piece /pi:s/ trozo
pig /pɪg/ cerdo
pillow /ˈpɪləʊ/ almohada
pitch /pɪtʃ/ campo
place /pleɪs/ lugar
plane /pleɪn/ avión

plaster /'plɑ:stə/ tirita
play /pleɪ/ tocar, obra de teatro
player /'pleɪə/ jugador, jugadora
please /pli:z/ por favor
pleased /pli:zd/ contento, satisfecho
plenty of /'plenti ɒv/ mucho(s)
plug into /'plʌg ɪntu:/ enchufar en
pocket /'pɒkɪt/ bolsillo
polar bear /'pəʊlə beə/ oso, osa polar
police officer /pə'li:s ɒfɪsə/ agente de policía
pond /pɒnd/ estanque
pool /pu:l/ piscina
poor /pɔ:: pʊə/ pobre
popular /'pɒpjələ/ popular, famoso
population /pɒpju'leɪʃn/ población
portable hard drive /pɔ:təbl 'hɑ:d draɪv/ disco duro extraíble
portion /'pɔ:ʃn/ ración
portrait /'pɔ:treɪt/ retrato
(by) post /pəʊst/ (por) correo
post office /'pəʊst ɒfɪs/ correos
postal worker /'pəʊstl wɜ:kə/ empleado, empleada de correos
postcard /'pəʊstkɑ:d/ postal
pottery /'pɒtəri/ cerámica
pound /paʊnd/ libra
poverty /'pɒvəti/ pobreza
power /'paʊə/ poder
prawn /prɔ:n/ gamba
present /'preznt/ regalo
pretend /prɪ'tend/ fingir
primary school /'praɪməri sku:l/ educación primaria
prince /prɪns/ príncipe
print /prɪnt/ imprimir
printer /'prɪntə/ impresora
prize /praɪz/ premio
profile /'prəʊfaɪl/ perfil
protect /prə'tekt/ proteger
pump /pʌmp/ bombear
punishment /'pʌnɪʃmənt/ castigo
put /pʊt/ poner
put down /pʊt 'daʊn/ dejar
put on /pʊt 'ɒn/ ponerse

Q

qualification /kwɒlɪfɪ'keɪʃn/ título
quality /'kwɒlɪti/ calidad
quantity /'kwɒntɪti/ cantidad
queen /kwi:n/ reina
question /'kwestʃən/ pregunta, preguntar
quick /kwɪk/ rápido
quick-witted /kwɪk'wɪtɪd/ agudo
quiet /'kwaɪət/ callado, tranquilo
quite /kwaɪt/ bastante
quiz /kwɪz/ juego de preguntas y respuestas

R

race /reɪs/ carrera
railroad /'reɪlrəʊd/ ferrocarril
rain /reɪn/ lluvia, llover
rainfall /'reɪnfɔ:l/ precipitaciones
rainforest /'reɪnfɒrɪst/ bosque tropical
rainy /'reɪni/ lluvioso
rate /reɪt/ valorar, puntuar
raw /rɔ:/ crudo
reach /ri:tʃ/ llegar a
ready /'redi/ preparado
realize /'rɪəlaɪz/ darse cuenta (de)
reason /'ri:zn/ razón
receipt /rɪ'si:t/ recibo
receive /rɪ'si:v/ recibir
recent /'ri:sənt/ reciente
recipe book /'resəpi: bʊk/ libro de recetas
recluse /rɪ'klu:s/ recluso, reclusa
refuse /rɪ'fju:z/ rechazar, negarse
relative /'relətɪv/ familiar
relax /rɪ'læks/ relajarse
reluctant /rɪ'lʌktənt/ reticente
rely on /rɪ'laɪ ɒn/ depender de
remain /rɪ'meɪn/ permanecer
remember /rɪ'membə/ recordar
remote control /rɪməʊt kən'trəʊl/ mando a distancia
replace /rɪ'pleɪs/ sustituir
report /rɪ'pɔ:t/ informe
request /rɪ'kwest/ petición
rescue /'reskju:/ rescate
resign /rɪ'zaɪn/ dimitir
rest /rest/ descanso, resto
resurrect /rezə'rekt/ resucitar
return /rɪ'tɜ:n/ volver
reveal /rɪ'vi:l/ revelar
revise /rɪ'vaɪz/ repasar
reward /rɪ'wɔ:d/ premio, recompensa
rice /raɪs/ arroz
rich /rɪtʃ/ rico
ride /raɪd/ paseo
right /raɪt/ bien, correcto
ring /rɪŋ/ sonar, llamar
ripe /raɪp/ maduro
risk /rɪsk/ arriesgarse (a), riesgo
river /'rɪvə/ río
road /rəʊd/ carretera
roasted /'rəʊstɪd/ asado
rob /rɒb/ robar
robbery /'rɒbəri/ robo
rock climbing /'rɒk klaɪmɪŋ/ escalar
roll /rəʊl/ rodar, estirar
rollerblading /'rəʊləbleɪdɪŋ/ andar con patines en línea
room /ru:m, rʊm/ habitación, espacio
rope /rəʊp/ cuerda
rough /rʌf/ áspero
round /raʊnd/ partida, asalto, alrededor de
rubbish /'rʌbɪʃ/ basura
rude /ru:d/ maleducado
run /rʌn/ correr
run away /rʌn ə'weɪ/ huir
run on /rʌn 'ɒn/ seguir corriendo
run out of /rʌn 'aʊt ɒv/ salir corriendo

S

sad /sæd/ triste
safe /seɪf/ seguro, a salvo
sailing boat /'seɪlɪŋ bəʊt/ barco de pesca
same /seɪm/ mismo
sane /seɪn/ cuerdo
sauce /sɔ:s/ salsa
sausage /'sɒsɪdʒ/ salchicha
save /seɪv/ grabar, salvar
say /seɪ/ decir
scale /skeɪl/ escalar
scared /skeəd/ asustado
scarf /skɑ:f/ pañuelo, bufanda
scary /'skeəri/ que da miedo
scenery /'si:nəri/ paisaje
scheme /ski:m/ proyecto
science /'saɪəns/ ciencias
scooter /'sku:tə/ vespa
score /skɔ:/ puntuación, resultado
scratch off /skrætʃ 'ɒf/ rascar
scream /skri:m/ gritar
screen /skri:n/ pantalla
sea /si:/ mar
season /'si:zn/ estación (del año)
seat /si:t/ asiento
secondary (school) /'sekəndri/ (educación) secundaria
secondly /'sekəndli/ en segundo lugar
see /si:/ ver
seem /si:m/ parecer
self-cleaning /self'kli:nɪŋ/ de limpieza automática
selfish /'selfɪʃ/ egoísta
sell /sel/ vender
send /send/ mandar, enviar
sensible /'sensəbl/ sensato
separate /'seprət/ distinto
serious /'sɪəriəs/ serio
several /'sevrəl/ varios
shallow /'ʃæləʊ/ superficial, no profundo
share /ʃeə/ compartir
shark /ʃɑ:k/ tiburón
sheep /ʃi:p/ oveja(s)
shelf /ʃelf/ balda, estante
shine /ʃaɪn/ brillar, lucir
ship /ʃɪp/ barco
shirt /ʃɜ:t/ camisa
shocked /ʃɒkt/ horrorizado
shoe /ʃu:/ zapato
shoot /ʃu:t/ disparar
shop /ʃɒp/ tienda
shop assistant /'ʃɒp əsɪstənt/ dependiente, dependienta
shoplifting /'ʃɒplɪftɪŋ/ robo (en tiendas)
short /ʃɔ:t/ corto
shortly /'ʃɔ:tli/ dentro de poco, en breve
shoulder /'ʃəʊldə/ hombro
shout /ʃaʊt/ gritar
show /ʃəʊ/ enseñar, mostrar, espectáculo, programa
shower /'ʃaʊə/ ducha
shy /ʃaɪ/ tímido
side /saɪd/ lado
signature /'sɪgnətʃə/ firma
significant /sɪg'nɪfɪkənt/ significativo
signpost /'saɪnpəʊst/ señal
silver /'sɪlvə/ (de) plata
since /sɪns/ desde (que)
sing /sɪŋ/ cantar
sister /'sɪstə/ hermana
sit down /sɪt 'daʊn/ sentarse
size /saɪz/ tamaño
skate /skeɪt/ patinar
skateboard /'skeɪtbɔ:d/ skate
ski /ski:/ esquiar
skill /skɪl/ destreza
skin /skɪn/ piel
sky /skaɪ/ cielo
sky dive /'skaɪ daɪv/ lanzarse en paracaídas (en caída libre)
skyscraper /'skaɪskreɪpə/ rascacielos
sleep /sli:p/ dormir
sleepover /'sli:pəʊvə/ pasar la noche fuera de casa
sleepy /'sli:pi/ adormilado
sleeve /sli:v/ manga
slice /slaɪs/ rodaja
slope /sləʊp/ inclinarse
small /smɔ:l/ pequeño
smart /smɑ:t/ elegante
smart tag /'smɑ:t tæg/ etiqueta inteligente
smell /smel/ olor
smile /smaɪl/ sonreír, sonrisa
smoke /sməʊk/ fumar
smooth /smu:ð/ suave
snorkelling /'snɔ:kəlɪŋ/ buceo
so that /'səʊ ðət/ así es que
sock /sɒk/ calcetín
soft /sɒft/ suave
solve /sɒlv/ resolver, solucionar
somebody /'sʌmbədi/ alguien
someone /'sʌmwʌn/ alguien
something else /sʌmθɪŋ 'els/ algo más
sometimes /'sʌmtaɪmz/ a veces
song /sɒŋ/ canción
soon /su:n/ pronto
sorry /'sɒri/ perdón
sound /saʊnd/ sonido
sound like /'saʊnd laɪk/ sonar
soup /su:p/ sopa
source /sɔ:s/ fuente
south /saʊθ/ sur
southwest /saʊθ'west/ suroeste
space /speɪs/ espacio
span /spæn/ ámbito
spare time /speə 'taɪm/ tiempo libre
speak /spi:k/ hablar
special /'speʃl/ especial
speech /spi:tʃ/ discurso
speeding /'spi:dɪŋ/ superar el límite de velocidad
spend /spend/ pasar (tiempo), gastar (dinero),
spill /spɪl/ derramar
spoil /spɔɪl/ estropear
spoonful /'spu:nfʊl/ cucharada
sport /spɔ:t/ deporte
spot /spɒt/ grano
spring /sprɪŋ/ primavera
square /skweə/ plaza, cuadrado
stairs /steəz/ escaleras
stall /stɔ:l/ puesto
stamp /stæmp/ sello
stand up /stænd 'ʌp/ levantarse
star /stɑ:/ estrella
start /stɑ:t/ empezar
state /steɪt/ estado

statement /'steɪtmənt/ declaración
stay /steɪ/ alojarse, quedarse
steak /steɪk/ chuleta
steal /sti:l/ robar
steel /sti:l/ acero
stewed /stju:d/ guisado
stick /stɪk/ pegarse
still /stɪl/ todavía
stone /stəʊn/ piedra
stop /stɒp/ parar
store /stɔ:/ almacenar, tienda
story /'stɔ:ri/ historia, narración
strange /streɪndʒ/ extraño
strawberry /'strɔ:bəri/ fresa
street /stri:t/ calle
strength /streŋθ/ fuerza
stressed /strest/ estresado
stretcher /'stretʃə/ camilla
stroke /strəʊk/ acariciar
strong /strɒŋ/ fuerte
style /staɪl/ estilo
subject /'sʌbdʒekt/ tema
successful /sʌk'sesfl/ de éxito
suddenly /sʌdənli/ de repente
sugar /'ʃugə/ azúcar
suggest /sə'dʒest/ sugerir
suit /su:t/ traje
summarize /'sʌməraɪz/ resumir
summer /'sʌmə/ verano
sun /sʌn/ sol
sunny /'sʌni/ soleado
supply /sə'plaɪ/ suministro
support /sə'pɔ:t/ apoyar, mantener
surely /'ʃʊəli, ʃɔ:li/ seguro
surf the Internet /sɜ:f ði 'ɪntənet/ navegar por Internet
surface /'sɜ:fɪs/ superficie
surprise /sə'praɪz/ sorpresa
survey /'sɜ:veɪ/ encuesta
sweep /swi:p/ barrer
sweet /swi:t/ caramelo
swim /swɪm/ nadar
swimming pool /'swɪmɪŋ pu:l/ piscina
switch /swɪtʃ/ cambio
sympathy /'sɪmpəθi/ compasión

T

table /'teɪbl/ mesa
take /teɪk/ llevar, tardarse
take off /teɪk 'ɒf/ quitarse
take part /teɪk 'pɑ:t/ tomar parte
take place /teɪk 'pleɪs/ celebrarse
takeaway /'teɪkəweɪ/ comida para llevar
talkative /'tɔ:kətɪv/ charlatán
tall /tɔ:l/ alto
taste /teɪst/ sabor
tea /ti:/ té
team /ti:m/ equipo
technology /tek'nɒlədʒi/ tecnología
teenager /'ti:neɪdʒə/ adolescente
teeth /ti:θ/ dientes
tell /tel/ decir, contar
temporary /'temprəri/ temporal
term /tɜ:m/ trimestre
terrible /'terɪbl/ horrible
test /test/ examinar, examen, test
textbook /'tekstbʊk/ libro de texto
theatre /'θɪətə/ teatro
theft /θeft/ robo
then /ðen/ entonces, después
there /ðeə/ ahí, allí
thief /θi:f/ ladrón, ladrona
thin /θin/ flaco
thing /θɪŋ/ cosa
think of /'θɪŋk ɒv/ pensar de, opinar sobre
(a) third /θɜ:d/ (un) tercio
(be) thirsty /'θɜ:sti/ (tener) sed
this /ðis/ este
thoughtful /'θɔ:tfl/ considerado
thousand /'θaʊzənd/ mil
throw /θrəʊ/ recoger
throw out /θrəʊ 'aʊt/ tirar
ticket /'tɪkɪt/ billete
tidy /'taɪdi/ ordenar, ordenado
time /taɪm/ rato, tiempo
tiny /'taɪni/ muy pequeño
tiptoe /'tɪptəʊ/ puntillas
tired /'taɪəd/ cansado
tiring /'taɪərɪŋ/ canso, que cansa
toast /təʊst/ tostada(s)
today /tə'deɪ/ hoy en día, en la actualidad
together /tə'geðə/ juntos
toilet /'tɔɪlət/ baño
tongue /tʌŋ/ lengua
too /tu:/ también, demasiado
tools /tu:lz/ herramientas
toothpaste /'tu:θpeɪst/ pasta de dientes
top /tɒp/ parte de arriba
topic /'tɒpɪk/ tema
tournament /'tʊənəmənt/ torneo, competición
towards /tə'wɔ:dz/ hacia
tower block /'taʊə blɒk/ bloque alto, torre de apartamentos
town /taʊn/ ciudad
town hall /taʊn 'hɔ:l/ ayuntamiento
toy /tɔɪ/ juguete
(MP3) track /træk/ pista (de MP3)
trade /treɪd/ comercio
train /treɪn/ tren, entrenar
trainers /'treɪnəz/ zapatillas de deporte
tram /træm/ tranvía
travel /'trævl/ viaje, viajar
tray /treɪ/ bandeja
treatment /'tri:tmənt/ tratamiento
trial /'traɪəl/ juicio
trolley /'trɒli/ carrito
trousers /'traʊzəz/ pantalones
true /tru:/ verdadero, verdad
try /traɪ/ intentar, probar
T-shirt /'ti:ʃɜ:t/ camiseta de manga corta
turkey /'tɜ:ki/ pavo
turn /tɜ:n/ darse la vuelta
turn around /tɜ:n ə'raʊnd/ volverse
turn off /tɜ:n 'ɒf/ apagar
turn on /tɜ:n 'ɒn/ encender
(TV) show /ti:'vi: ʃəʊ/ programa (de la tele)
twice /twaɪs/ dos veces
twin /twɪn/ mellizo
typically /'tɪpɪkli/ normalmentee

U

ugly /'ʌgli/ feo
ultimate /'ʌltɪmət/ definitivo, mejor
umbrella /ʌm'brelə/ paraguas
uncle /'ʌŋkl/ tío
under /'ʌndə/ bajo
underneath /ʌndə'ni:θ/ debajo
understand /ʌndə'sθænd/ entender
unfortunately /ʌn'fɔ:tʃənətli/ desgraciadamente
unhealthy /ʌn'helθi/ poco sano
UK /ju:'keɪ/ Reino Unido
United States (US) /ju:naɪtɪd 'steɪts/ Estados Unidos (EEUU)
unofficial /ʌnə'fɪʃl/ no oficial
unripe /ʌn'raɪp/ verde, no maduro
untidy /ʌn'taɪdi/ descuidado
until /ʌn'tɪl/ hasta
up to /'ʌp tu:/ hasta
upset /ʌp'set/ disgustado
upside-down /ʌpsaɪd'daʊn/ boca abajo
upstairs /ʌp'steəz/ arriba
USB hub /ju:es'bi: hʌb/ dispositivo para conectar varios USBs
use /ju:z/ utilizar, uso
useless /'ju:sləs/ inútil
usually /'ju:ʒuəli/ generalmente

V

vacuum cleaner /'vækju:m kli:nə/ aspirador
valley /'væli/ valle
valuable /'væljuəbl/ valioso
vanilla /və'nɪlə/ vainilla
vase /vɑ:z/ jarrón
venue /'venju:/ escenario
very /'veri/ muy
view /vju:/ vista, opinión
village /'vɪlɪdʒ/ pueblecito
volleyball /'vɒlibɔ:l/ voleibol
vote /vəʊt/ votar

W

wait /weɪt/ esperar
waiter /'weɪtə/ camarero
walk /wɔ:k/ paseo
wall /wɔ:l/ pared, muro
walnut /'wɔ:lnʌt/ nuez
wander /'wɒndə/ andar sin rumbo
wardrobe /'wɔ:drəʊb/ armario ropero
warm /wɔ:m/ caliente
warning /'wɔ:nɪŋ/ aviso
wash up /wɒʃ 'ʌp/ lavar
washing /'wɒʃɪŋ/ colada
washing machine /'wɒʃɪŋ məʃi:n/ lavadora
waste /weɪst/ desperdicio
watch /wɒtʃ/ reloj de pulsera, ver
water /'wɔ:tə/ agua
waterfall /'wɔ:təfɔ:l/ cascada
waterskiing /'wɔ:təski:ɪŋ/ esquí acuático
way /weɪ/ manera
weak /wi:k/ débil
wealthy /'welθi/ adinerado
wear /weə/ llevar (puesto), vestir
weather /'weðə/ tiempo meteorológico
weather forecast /'weðə fɔ:kɑ:st/ pronóstico del tiempo
web cam /'web kæm/ cámara web
weekday /'wi:kdeɪ/ día de la semana
weekend /wi:k'end/ fin de semana
weigh /weɪ/ pesar
weird /wɪəd/ raro, extraño
well /wel/ bien, bueno
well-known /wel 'nəʊn/ conocido, famoso
west /west/ oeste
wet /wet/ mojado, húmedo
whale /weɪl/ ballena
what? /wɒt/ ¿qué?
whatever /wɒt'evə/ cualquier
wheel /wi:l/ rueda
when /wen/ cuando
where /weə/ donde
while /waɪl/ mientras que
(a) while /waɪl/ (un) rato
whistle /'wɪsl/ silbar
whole /həʊl/ entero
wide /waɪd/ ancho
wife /waɪf/ mujer, esposa
win /wɪn/ ganar
wind /wɪnd/ viento
window /'wɪndəʊ/ ventana
wine /waɪn/ vino
wireless headset /waɪələs 'hedset/ auriculares inalámbricos
without /wɪ'ðaʊt/ sin
witness /'wɪtnəs/ testigo
woman, women /'wʊmən/ /'wɪmɪn/ mujer, mujeres
wonder /'wʌndə/ preguntarse
wonderful /'wʌndəfl/ maravilloso
wood /wʊd/ madera
word /wɜ:d/ palabra
work /wɜ:k/ trabajar, funcionar, trabajo
workhouse /'wɜ:khaʊs/ especie de fábrica para gente pobre
world /wɜ:ld/ mundo
worried /wʌrid/ preocupado
worse /wɜ:s/ peor
worth /wɜ:θ/ que vale/n
write /raɪt/ escribir

Y

year /jɪə/ año
yesterday /'jestədeɪ/ ayer
young /jʌŋ/ joven

Expression Bank

A different kind of	Otro tipo de
Absolutely!	¡Desde luego!
After that	A continuación
Anything to drink?	¿Algo para beber?
At eight o'clock	A las ocho en punto
At midday	Al mediodía
Can I help you?	¿Puedo ayudarte?
Certainly	Por supuesto No faltaba más
Do you agree or disagree?	¿Estás de acuerdo o en desacuerdo?
Do you want to come?	¿Quieres venir?
Dress code	Código de indumentaria
Eventually	Al final
Finally	Finalmente
Fine, thanks	Bien, gracias
First of all	En primer lugar
Great!	¡Genial!
Guess what	Adivina
Here's your change	Aquí tienes tu cambio
Hey!	¡Eh!
Hi	Hola
How about you?	Y tú, ¿qué?
How about...?	¿Qué te parece...?
How are you?	¿Cómo estás?
How disappointing!	¡Qué decepcionante!
How embarrassing!	¡Qué embarazoso!
I don't believe it	No me lo creo
I don't think so	No lo creo
I hope	Espero que
I'd love to	Me encantaría
I'd love to try	Me encantaría probar
I'll text you	Te enviaré un SMS
I'm (not) really into	(No) me va
I'm a big fan of	Soy un gran fan de
I'm having a great time	Lo estoy pasando genial
I'm Lily	Soy Lily Me llamo Lily
I'm mad about	Me chifla Estoy loco por
I'm quite interested in	Me interesa bastante
I'm sorry	Lo siento
I'm very keen on	Soy muy aficionado a
In fact	De hecho
In the morning	Por la mañana
In the summer	En verano
Is it true?	¿Es cierto?
It's their fault	Es culpa suya
It's not their fault	No es culpa suya
It looks really fun	Parece muy divertido
It was his / her own fault	Fue culpa suya
It's a joke!	¡Estás de broma!
It's right to	Es apropiado Es correcto
It's too late	Es demasiado tarde
It's warm	Hace calor
Look!	¡Mira!
Maybe next year!	¡Quizá el año que viene!
Me too	Yo también
Not really	En realidad, no
OK!	¡Vale!
On Saturday afternoon	El sábado por la tarde
On Saturday evening	El sábado por la noche
On Saturday morning	El sábado por la mañana
Poor (Maria)	Pobre (Maria)
Really funny!	¡Qué divertido!
Really?	¿De verdad?
See you soon	Nos vemos pronto
See you there!	¡Nos vemso allí!
Singles event	Partido individual
Sit down	Siéntate Sentaos.
Sure	Seguro Por supuesto
Take turns	Hacedlo por turnos Turnaos
Thank you	Gracias
Thanks!	¡Gracias!
That's a shame	Es una lástima
That's good advice	Es un buen consejo
That's great news!	¡Qué buenas noticias!
What a great story!	¡Qué historia más genial!
What about you?	Y tú, ¿qué?
What about...?	¿Qué te parece...?
What time does it start?	¿A qué hora empieza?
What was it like?	¿Qué tal fue?
What was the weather like?	¿Qué tiempo hacía?
What's the problem?	¿Cuál es el problema?
What's your name?	¿Cómo te llamas?
Where do they take place?	¿Dónde tienen lugar?
Why don't we / you...?	¿Por qué no...?
Would you like to come?	¿Te gustaría venir?
Write soon	Escribe pronto